BUY NOW

The Ultimate Guide to Owning and Investing in Property

LLOYD EDGE

Bestselling author of *Positively Geared*

WILEY

First published in 2022 by John Wiley & Sons Australia, Ltd

42 McDougall St, Milton Qld 4064
Office also in Melbourne

Typeset in Garamond Premier Pro 12pt/15pt

© John Wiley & Sons Australia, Ltd 2022

The moral rights of the author have been asserted.

ISBN: 978-0-730-39523-2

A catalogue record for this book is available from the National Library of Australia

Cover design by Wiley
Cover image: © Scar1984 / Getty Images
Back cover author photo: Cathy Tiddy, Diamond Portraits
Internal icons: © Happy Art/Shutterstock

Disclaimer

To Caelen.

The world is what you build it to be.

CONTENTS

CONTENTS

ABOUT THE AUTHOR

Lloyd Edge (Dip. Prop. S, LREA, Licenced Buyer's Agent) is the founder and Managing Director of one of Australia's most sought after buyer's agencies, Aus Property Professionals.

He is the author of bestseller, *Positively Geared*, a book about his journey from high school teacher to building a multi-million dollar property portfolio and achieving financial independence while still on a teacher's salary.

'Property became my passion when I realised that it can be a vehicle to financial independence. Achieving capital growth while maintaining cash flow is essential to portfolio growth and ultimate financial independence'

Lloyd has achieved his goals, accumulating a property portfolio worth over $15 million that is cash flow positive, and he now lives in a beautiful waterfront home with his wife Renee and two sons, Riley and Caelen.

For Lloyd, work is now a choice. His investment strategies allowed him to retire from the rat race and he now helps clients achieve their own financial and lifestyle goals through property.

Lloyd has a diverse range of investment strategies to offer clients and readers alike. Where *Positively Geared* offers a step-by-step guide to achieving equity gains through building duplexes, Lloyd's second book, *Buy Now* offers multiple strategies for home buyers and first time investors.

He is often featured on TV for his comments on the property markets. He also has a regular segment on Geelong's Bay FM Property Guide, Sydney's Edge 96.1 and Perth's 6PR as well as a being a regular contributor to *Australian Property Investor* magazine. Lloyd is also often interviewed on top rating radio stations 2GB, 4BC and 3AW.

As a member of the Real Estate Buyer's Agents Association (REBAA), he has been a frequent finalist in the REINSW awards for excellence and Real Estate Business (REB) awards. Lloyd has received 'Your Investment Property' Top Buyer's Agent award and his company, Aus Property Professionals, has also been a finalist in these awards on a number of occasions. In 2020 Lloyd's first book, *Positively Geared* won an award in the Australian Business Book Awards (ABBA).

Industry accolades for Aus Property Professionals include (at time of publication):

- 2021 – Real Estate Business Awards: Aus Property Professionals, finalist, Buyer's Agency of the year.

- 2020 – REINSW Awards for Excellence: Lloyd Edge, finalist, Buyer's Agent of the year

- 2020 – REINSW Awards for Excellence: Aus Property Professionals, finalist, Buyer's Agency of the Year.

- 2020 – Real Estate Business Awards: Lloyd Edge, finalist, Buyer's Agent of the year

- 2020 – Real Estate Business Awards: Aus Property Professsionals, finalist, Buyer's Agency of the year

- 2020 – Australian Business Book Awards: Winner, *Positively Geared*, best marketing and publicity.

- 2019 – Real Estate Business Awards: Lloyd Edge, finalist, Buyer's Agent of the year

- 2019 – Real Estate Business Awards: Aus Property Professionals, finalist, Buyer's Agency of the year.

- 2019 – REINSW Awards for Excellence: Renee Edge, finalist, Operational Support

- 2019 – REINSW Awards for Excellence: Lloyd Edge, finalist, Buyer's Agent of the year

- 2019 – REINSW Awards for Excellence: Aus Property Professionals, finalist, Buyer's Agency of the Year.

- 2018 – REINSW Awards for Excellence: Aus Property Professionals, finalist, Buyer's Agency of the Year

- 2018 – REINSW Awards for Excellence: Aus Property Professsionals, finalist, Buyer's Agency of the year

- 2018 – REINSW Awards for Excellence: Renee Edge, Winner, Operational Support

- 2018 – Property Investor Awards, *Your Investment Property magazine:* Lloyd Edge, Top Buyer's Agent (ranked first in NSW, third in Australia).

- 2017 – REINSW Awards for Excellence: Lloyd Edge, finalist, Buyer's Agent of the year

ACKNOWLEDGEMENTS

My wife Renee told me that I must not write another book this year. We were having our second child, along with having a toddler at home, my business was continuing to grow which was keeping me busy, and we were in the middle of a pandemic. She insisted this was NOT the year to write another book. So I decided that I must go ahead and produce another book. So, thanks Renee for having the confidence in me!

Anna Warwick has worked with me on *Buy Now* as my developmental editor and I can't thank her enough for her work and support. You're tremendous. Thanks Anna!

I would also like to thank the team at Wiley who approached me to produce another book following the tremendous success of *Positively Geared*.

To my staff at Aus Property Professionals, thank you for your fantastic work and support in the business.

I would also like to take this opportunity to thank you, the readers for picking up *Buy Now* and I hope you find some gold nuggets that will help you along in your own journey in property.

INTRODUCTION
WHY BUY NOW?

This book is for first-time property investors and first home buyers and for those considering their first or next step. It will help you understand how to find your first home or investment property, how to budget for it and how to read the markets.

ON HELP – GIVING AND RECEIVING

My role as a buyer's agent is essentially to help people, and I take this role very seriously. Yet, after many years' experience, I'm still amazed and inspired when my advice and example help give my clients a new perspective, opening up a world of opportunity they'd only dreamed about.

The media is full of noise about high property values, and how first home buyers can never break into this 'unaffordable' market. But it isn't true. There are always ways to manage it. If you can't afford a property where you want to buy right now, as you'll read in *Buy Now*, there are all sorts of strategies you can deploy to build the equity you need to be able to buy the home you want down the track. But this doesn't mean putting things off.

LLOYD'S STRATEGY

BUY NOW. I never advocate waiting to buy: I don't think anyone ever got ahead by waiting.

Of course it can be difficult initially to break into the property market, and some people find it hard to ask for help. They don't know who to believe, what advice to take and what will work for them. New clients come to me and share their frustration: they feel they've done everything they can and are still getting nowhere. They're working long hours and not spending enough time with the kids. They have a home, but they've got a big mortgage on it, and they're trying to work out how they're ever going to pay it off before retirement. Because, let's face it, if it's going to take you 30 years to pay it off, how will you ever be able to afford your dream home?

Even clients who own a really nice property feel like they're stuck. One I recall was living in the Sydney suburb of Burraneer, quite close to where I live. He had a beautiful house, but the $1.8 million mortgage on it was killing him.

After coming to me for advice, he sold that beautiful home and moved into a rental so he could invest his equity into doing some developments. I helped him build a duplex, which he's making a huge profit on. Now that client is looking towards his next development.

And best of all, he's now living debt-free.

THE IMPORTANCE OF STRATEGY

At some point everyone needs a mentor — someone with hands-on experience to help them get on track. I didn't start out with a strategy. If I'd had someone to advise me from the beginning, I probably would have done better, faster. My own experiences, both positive and negative, have helped me set up my clients strategically far better than I was, and I look at some of those in chapter 6.

At the time, I simply wanted to buy a principal place of residence, and if that's what you want as well, I cover it in chapter 4.

But if I'd had a strategy back then, I probably wouldn't have started out by buying that unit in Rockdale (more on this in chapter 1). I definitely wouldn't have lived in it. Instead, I would have 'rentvested' and built up a portfolio faster. And I would have started investing when I was younger but, of course, I didn't know any of this back then. A mentor might have advised me, 'Don't buy a home to live in — just invest'. Who knows? I might have been advised to buy Rockdale anyway. Being close to amenities and close to the water, it was a sound investment (albeit an accidental one). All I know is I had no strategy, because I didn't know what I was trying to achieve. I didn't have a clear goal.

In fact, I wasn't happy with my first few properties, because in those days I had quite a bit of debt. Those properties were negatively geared, and it frustrated me because I wanted to *create money* through property. So you see, even after I'd started buying investment properties, I didn't know what I was doing.

That was almost 20 years ago. Today I've achieved a lot of what I set out to do. My goals included buying my dream home (I cover that in chapter 5) and building security for my family. I have a strategy in place for how to pay my property off through my investments. I no longer dream of what I want to achieve in the property markets. I've got other dreams, but they're a little different.

My advice to my clients is not predicated on a hypothetical strategy, but on long experience helping hundreds of clients each year work towards achieving their own goals. That's what's important. It's about achieving your big goals and enjoying life to the full.

AN INDEPENDENT INCOME

Everyone needs a roof over their head, but that's not the only reason to focus on property. Today we can see just how important it is to be able to control our own income. Even in times of crisis, when job security goes out the window, property will continue to generate a passive income, which is why it remains the safest and most effective way to shore up your income and lifestyle goals.

But to really make it work for you, you first need to understand *why* you're investing. Everyone gets into property for a different reason. For many, particularly investors, it's to try to build wealth and set themselves up financially.

Many of my clients start out without a strategy. They don't know where or what to buy, and they underestimate how much a property will actually cost. So for every client who walks through my door, the process starts with *goal-setting* (more on this in chapter 1). This is a vital first step because, before you create your property investment strategy, you need a reason to begin investing, and you need an objective that motivates you to stick to it.

Think about where you would like to be in 10, 15 or 20 years' time. Once you have your end goal in mind, you can begin working on strategy and finance, and taking the steps needed to build up a property portfolio and achieve that ultimate long-term goal — financial freedom. We'll get into all of that in this book.

THE TRIFECTA STRATEGY

Fifteen years ago I was a full-time music teacher on an income of less than $70 000, still paying off that one-bedroom unit in Rockdale, and I realised that if I kept doing what I was doing, I was never going to achieve my goal of securing my dream home.

I could see that negative gearing was going to keep me at work forever, because I was subsidising the mortgage through my income and waiting — potentially for decades — for capital growth.

So I looked into ways to create *positively geared* investments and bought a high-cashflow rental property in a mining town, which lost most of its value and rental income when the resources market bottomed out. I've never made that mistake again!

Now I research the markets for *high-growth* properties with good rental demand in areas with multiple stable economic drivers. I'll cover this in chapter 10.

When investing in property, I also look for ways I can 'manufacture equity' rather than relying solely on the organic growth of the markets.

Manufacturing equity might mean anything from a cosmetic to a structural renovation to boost the value and rental yield of a property. We will explore how to create your own equity in chapter 7, and cover this renovation strategy in depth in chapter 8.

While you might be priced out of the markets in the capital cities (we cover reading the markets in chapter 9), there are still many properties available across the country that you can buy, subdivide and then sell off the backyard (known as a battle-axe lot). These properties can offer a great cashflow injection for your portfolio. I did this a few times while building my portfolio.

The investment strategy that really launched my property portfolio like a rocket came through my discovery of *the power of building duplexes*. When I built my first duplex and subdivided it, I made twice as much in equity as I earned in a whole year from teaching.

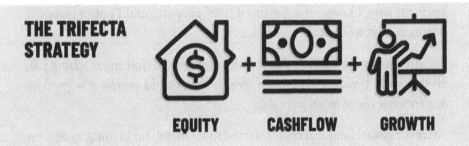

THE TRIFECTA STRATEGY — EQUITY + CASHFLOW + GROWTH

After this *aha* moment, I started to acquire several properties a year, just using equity and manufacturing capital growth instead of waiting for capital growth to occur organically. I have regularly seen this strategy create upwards of $200 000 in manufactured equity as well as providing positive cashflow through the dual income.

Doing this allowed me to take control of where my portfolio was heading and accelerate that growth. This meant my portfolio was growing, regardless of what the markets did.

The real power of the trifecta strategy is that you're able to manufacture instant equity then hold properties as they earn you more money than you're spending. By holding these properties over long periods of time, you'll also benefit from their ongoing capital growth.

Better still, it's a process you can 'rinse and repeat'. By using my trifecta strategy, you can very quickly grow your property portfolio and your income, and before long you'll find yourself among the 1 per cent of Australians who hold more than five investment properties.

And best of all, those properties will be earning you an income in the process.

WHERE INVESTMENT HAS TAKEN ME

Fast forward 15 years, and I now own a $15 million property portfolio and live in my dream home.

The main underlying reason I was able to achieve this was because I knew my *why*. I knew what I wanted from property and I put in place the strategies that would take me there.

I wanted a passive income that would allow me to quit my teaching job, all the while building long-term wealth that would *continue to grow no matter what the markets were doing*.

After the global financial crisis I started to set myself up to mitigate against future major economic downturns. (I wonder why more people don't do the same.) For me, this meant first educating myself, with many nights spent studying and researching the property markets while working at my teaching job during the day. In less than 10 years, at the age of 40, my positively geared portfolio had replaced my income and I was able to retire from teaching. A couple of years after that my wife Renee and I bought our dream home.

Most people are too fearful to leave a secure job to follow their dream. But if you build up a positively geared property portfolio that pretty much looks after itself, then you no longer need to rely on another source of income because *the investments are paying you an income*.

I am now truly financially free.

I have my own business as well. The two income streams, from my property portfolio and my buyer's agency business, offer me more security than I could hope for, compared to a job where at any point the boss could say, 'We don't need you anymore'.

And every day I help my clients pursue similar strategies. Throughout this book you'll find real-life case studies that illustrate what you can do to pursue your own goals.

STARTING OUT

Maybe you picked up this book because you're ready to buy a home. Or perhaps you can't afford to buy where you want to live, so you're looking for investment options to build equity.

You may be afraid to borrow money to invest. You can mitigate the risk by doing your due diligence (discussed in chapter 10), and by always buying in an area with low vacancy rates and lots of demand. That way you'll be sure to find tenants. In almost 20 years as an investor, I've rarely had trouble finding tenants for my residential properties.

If you're just starting your investment portfolio, you could look at a capital city like Adelaide, for example, or a strong regional city such as Orange or Toowoomba, where you can still find yourself a property for $450 000 or $500 000. With a 10 per cent deposit plus stamp duty and legal costs, you could get into that property for as little as $60 000 to $70 000.

If you're already a property owner and you've saved up a bit of money by putting extra into your existing mortgage, you can redraw that equity from an offset account and look at using it to get into another property. That's a great way of looking at things, and I go into it in more detail in chapter 3.

I spent years learning how to invest, but by sharing the strategies I learned the hard way, this book will help you get started right away.

Aside from leverage, which I'll talk about in chapter 3, the other fantastic thing about investing in property and applying different strategies to suit your various properties is that, even though you're essentially creating a physical asset, you can remain pretty 'hands-off' in the process.

I started investing while still teaching full-time. Later, when I had retired from the nine-to-five, I set up my buyer's agency business. So I wasn't researching properties for myself 24/7. I was doing enough research to find the right investment property; then once I'd bought it and put tenants in, I'd have a property manager managing those tenants and the property.

Buying and developing property involves enlisting a team of experts, like a property manager, from diverse fields. I call them my 'dream team' (more on them in chapter 2).

The dream team is there to help you successfully finance and purchase properties, and meet a multitude of legal and practical requirements, on time and within budget.

You need to do all the due diligence on the property you want to buy, but once you've signed the contract, you bring in professionals to look after it and you move on. You appoint a property manager, who will find and look after the tenants. If you're building a duplex, it's essential to have the right builder on board for what ideally should be a stress-free and largely hands-off process.

It's vitally important that you work with people you can trust to act in your best interests. When you surround yourself with reliable professionals, you can find yourself using them over multiple projects spanning many years as you build your property portfolio.

Nowadays I hardly ever hear from my property managers unless a particular problem arises, because they look after everything. So it's out of sight, out of mind. With trustworthy people looking after it, your portfolio pretty much runs itself.

So yes, even in your busy life, *you do have time for this*. By the time you've read this book, I'm confident I will have convinced you that you have nothing to lose by taking the plunge. There's really nothing stopping you from getting ready to *buy now*.

CHAPTER 1
THE POWER OF WHY

To get it, you must know why you want it

 I have built a large property portfolio, with assets, valued at $15 million, spread across three states. In this chapter I'll explain how I set goals when I began my property journey, including buying my first home and upgrading to my second, and how I learned to build a strategy with a long-term focus.

As I've noted, for me it didn't happen overnight — it took 15 years. Could I have done it any faster? Yes. I made some mistakes early on that set me back. That's why I wrote this book — to show you how to create and meet your investment goals *without* making those rookie mistakes. In fact, it took me less than 10 years once I actually had a strategy in place and put my mind to it. So my main message is simple: if I can do it, so can you.

Over the past two centuries about 90 per cent of the world's millionaires have made their millions by investing in real estate. When it comes to creating wealth through property, however, it is not about going out and buying just any property, then sitting and waiting for your wealth to build. It is a long game — one that you plan and work for one step at a time. It involves psychology and a strong belief — it's something you must *really want*.

What I came to realise in my early career as a property investor was that all successful investors have personal goals to track their successes, and that they grow their portfolios steadily based on long-term strategic plans. With that kind of long-term focus, strategic investors can buy more properties, enjoy greater serviceability and create greater wealth over time.

GOAL-SETTING

I was fortunate in that I was already a goal-setter. From my background as both a musician and a golfer, I knew how to set goals and meet them through hard work and determination. So forming a strategy was the natural next step for me. And it worked.

Looking back over 20 years, and especially the past 10 to 15 years, I always set myself goals. For example, 'In five years' time I want to have built this much wealth' or 'In 10 years' time I want to retire from teaching, and these are the investment strategies I'll use to achieve that' or 'I want to get my real-estate diploma in one year instead of three'. And I held myself accountable for those goals and strategies.

In fact, through my determination and willingness to work all hours of the night while holding down a full-time job, I gained my Diploma in Property in just three months.

I'm not suggesting that everyone should follow in my footsteps and buy 15, 20, 30 properties. Nor is it my advice that you should set your sights on becoming a multimillionaire — your goals may not run to that. What I'm talking about (and I'll share plenty of real-life illustrations in this book) is that you pursue your own goals, which might mean a strategy that you build a nest egg of three or four properties. If they're cashflow positive and see good capital growth, they should provide you with a steady income stream to fall back on if you lose your job or your business is shut down or you get sick and can't work.

You need to be clear on your *reasons* for taking this journey as well as the *belief* that you can do it — and you need to start developing both as early as you can.

LIFESTYLE CHOICES

I own a buyer's agency called Aus Property Professionals, but being a buyer's agent isn't really what I do, and it's not what I tell people I do. What I offer my clients is the means to achieve an *outcome*, which is the end goal they themselves have identified. So when people ask me what I do, I tell them I actually create lifestyle choices for people by helping them to create the equity that will eventually allow them to realise their dreams.

This is about much more than buying property. From my perspective, property is just the vehicle. Property, the stock market, gold or oil — they're all just vehicles. It's the outcome that's important.

Success comes down to really *knowing your why* — what you're trying to achieve. What are your goals in life? What sorts of lifestyle choices do you want to be able to make in the future? Once you're clear on the truly important things, then we can talk about crafting a strategy to enable you to achieve those goals through property.

Clients often come to me not really knowing what they want or why they want it. They may have been to a couple of property seminars, but they haven't taken the plunge yet. They may say, 'Yeah, I want to enjoy financial freedom through property' or 'I just want to grow a property portfolio'. I can tell you from firsthand experience that building a property portfolio is useless unless you know what it is going to achieve for you. How many properties do you want? More importantly, *why*? If financial independence is your key goal, what does that even look like for you?

Scan the QR code for a spreadsheet to help you set your goals.

These days I start the conversation by asking a lot of questions about my clients' motivations to get them thinking. Do you have kids? Do you want kids? Do you need extra funds to pay for their education or to be able to afford an annual family holiday without worrying about where the money is going to come from? Do you have a home mortgage? Is owning your home mortgage-free important for you, or are you aiming for your dream home and the ability to pay that off? And I have them put it all down on paper.

Working through all those ideas, and thinking about the *whys* that drive your life now and those you want to drive your future, will move your understanding one step forward. If you've never asked yourself these questions, the answers will give you the clarity you need to move in the right direction. When you know what you want, you become clearer about what you don't want.

If you have a goal of, say, $100 000 a year in passive income, or paying off your home mortgage, or putting your kids through a private-school education, we can work out how to deliver that and build a roadmap around that. Then we can start formulating the strategy that will get you there.

GOAL VS STRATEGY

A goal is an objective or destination. It could be paying off a mortgage, achieving financial freedom or buying a dream home. Smaller, interim goals (sometimes called momentum goals), such as saving for a family holiday or completing a duplex development, can be seen as milestones or stepping-stones on the path to success.

A strategy is a long-term plan for *how* you will achieve your goals. Those goals will determine your investment strategy—for example, whether the properties in your portfolio will be high-growth, instant equity, high-yield or subdivision projects. Without a strategy in place, there's a risk that you'll purchase the wrong type of property, one that doesn't help you achieve your goals.

Achieving financial freedom is a long-term process. The only strategy almost guaranteeing a fast result is the one in which you purchase your own home, because once we set the full purchase brief for that, we can obviously start the property-buying process pretty much right away. But most of our work is with long-term, repeat clients, because we have a long-term strategy in place that is about delivering the outcomes they want through investment after investment. This usually includes purchasing their own home as part of a longer property journey.

REALISTIC AND ATTAINABLE GOALS

Many people come to me with unrealistic goals. They want to invest in property for five years and within that time frame achieve a passive income of $300 000, or to be able to buy a $5 million home even though they have yet to start investing and have only a modest income!

Your goals need to be realistically achievable, because purchasing property always comes down to realistic planning, as I'll detail over the course of this book.

SMART GOAL-SETTING

Your goals define where you are heading and what you aim to achieve. For this reason, it is important to set both short-term and long-term goals.

Use the 'SMART' criteria:

 Specific. Ensure your goals are clear.

 Measured. Ensure your goals specify actual numbers or outcomes.

 Attainable. Do your research and your sums to make sure your goals are achievable.

 Realistic. Ask yourself whether your expectations are realistic.

 Time frame. Set a clear time frame for how long it will it take to achieve your goals.

Once you have set your goals, it's important to write them down. Equally important is to review your goals regularly to ensure you are consistently heading on the right track.

I tend to divide my goals into short-term, medium-term and long-term goals. This keeps me accountable. Achieving the 'momentum goals' in the short or medium term gives me a dopamine rush that allows me to move on to the next goal with greater confidence. Your long-term goals seem so much more accomplishable when you can see smaller goals being achieved in the short and medium term.

DEALING WITH UNCERTAINTY

I often emphasise the importance of enjoying the journey. You can't always be focusing on enjoying life in 10 or 15 years' time, when at last you get to buy that dream home. You need to enjoy life *now*, and to keep your goals fluid. For example, when the COVID-19 pandemic hit Australia in 2020, it became more difficult for some to buy the properties they wanted. With the goalposts shifting and even the banks working differently, people needed flexible plans. So set your long-term goals, but remain open to changes in external conditions. And be sure to enjoy the journey.

Another aphorism I like to share is this: if you're the smartest person in the room, you're in the wrong room. Surround yourself with people who can add more value to your practice than you alone can. It's really important to keep learning throughout life.

Don't take advice from people who haven't done what you're struggling to achieve. Instead, seek out people who have already accomplished your goals, and more. For example, don't use a buyer's agent who hasn't built up a property portfolio for themselves. That's not going to work for you.

I've made lots of mistakes along the way, and I'm happy to share this with my clients as well as in my writing and through the media. When clients approach me, I'll tell them quite openly, 'We're not going to go out and buy a property tomorrow. First we need to look at your why, to find out what you're hoping to achieve. Then we can develop a strategy that recognises how you can get there. Buying the property comes later'.

NO SILVER SPOONS HERE

A lot of my underlying principles, like being a straight shooter, relate to my own story. My parents gave me and my brother everything we wanted that they could afford, but we were always on a budget. There was only so much to spend on groceries each week, and snacks were limited luxuries. I'm sure that was a good thing! Holidays too were on a budget.

I was fortunate to go to a private school. My grandparents had sold their orchard when they retired and put money aside for their grandkids' education. If it weren't for them, I would not have had the sort of education I did.

So, looking back, I am aware that I've set things up differently because of this early experience. Financially, providing well for my own kids has always been an important goal. That was a big 'why' for me when I got serious about investing.

I have two sons: Riley was born in 2019 and Caelen in 2021. So I'm a dad now, and the world has changed a lot since I was a kid. Growing up on a farm in Orange in central New South Wales, I had plenty of freedom. I used to ride my bike everywhere during the day. I'd ride into town and ride 8 kilometres to school.

These days you need to be so careful about what your kids are up to, while trying not to become 'helicopter parents'. It's still early days for us as parents, and we recognise it will get more difficult to protect them from things like the influence of social media as they're growing up.

I can already appreciate the pressures on a lot of parents who feel they have to 'keep up' with other parents. Some spend thousands on kids' toys and clothes, even when they're struggling to pay the mortgage. Some kids wear these really nice clothes to day care, while Riley rocks up in his old workaday clothes. He may look a bit daggy, but he's just going to get paint and mud on them anyway!

People know we have a nice house and drive nice cars, but Caelen is still happy to play with a box. Riley's favourite toy is a five-dollar plastic lawnmower we bought second-hand on Facebook.

There's a front room on the second level at our place overlooking the Port Hacking estuary. Riley has his breakfast there because there's a cheap little table set up perfectly for him, and he loves that; in fact he insists on eating there. Of course, he has little to compare it with yet.

I've learned a lot about the importance for my clients of buying in school catchment zones, but we bought in this area simply because we loved the house. The local primary school is pretty good, by all accounts, so that's where my sons are going. We've booked them into a private school from year five or year seven, whichever works out.

I want my sons to treat others as they would want to be treated themselves, because that's how I like to treat people and that's how I was brought up. For me, teaching them to behave with honesty, integrity and humility is vital. I want them to be really accepting and to go to school with kids from all types of backgrounds and financial circumstances, where they can share what they have with others with humility.

What's important to me as a father is that Riley and Caelen are happy with what they are doing. People ask me, 'Are your kids going to take over your business some day?' They may, but then again they may not. But I *will* give them a good grounding on investing and looking after money — subjects they'll learn little about in school. Each of my boys will have a good financial head on his shoulders.

I had to learn all that the hard way.

MY PROPERTY GOALS

When I was a kid, long before I became the owner of a large, multi-faceted business, my first goal was to become a musician. And when I became a musician I had little money, because music is definitely not a well-paid profession.

I achieved one of my biggest life goals at the time when I moved to Sydney to study at the Sydney Conservatorium of Music. I loved studying, and I was doing some gigs and tutoring schoolkids in music to subsidise my AusStudy fees, which were like a government allowance for students in the 1990s.

In those days investing was the last thing on my mind, which in hindsight is pretty strange considering economics was actually my best subject at school. But I could see I wasn't going to make enough money as a teacher and musician. I used to run out of cash every fortnight. I remember one time I had to go to Newcastle for a music competition and didn't have a cent in my bank account, and couldn't even pay for petrol for the car. I was about 20 years old and I thought, this isn't the way I want to be living.

GOAL 1: SAVING TO BUY MY FIRST HOME

That realisation planted the seed of a financial goal. I thought, I have to start saving and putting money away.

And save I did. I was very frugal. I had no credit cards, though I drove a petrol-guzzling 1979 XD Ford Falcon. To keep a promise I'd made to myself, I didn't even travel overseas until after I'd bought my first property.

In my twenties I started to get interested in buying a property, not as an investment but so I didn't have to pay rent! I thought of rent as 'dead money', because that was what most of society believed back then.

Then, in 2003, I bought my first property, a tiny apartment of around 50 square metres in the southern Sydney suburb of Rockdale. I had saved up about $30 000, which covered the deposit and purchase costs.

I had no idea what I was doing really. It was the first time I had dealt with pushy real estate agents, and they must have seen me coming from a mile off. It was also my first experience working with a mortgage broker — which was actually fantastic, because I needed the personal assistance of a broker rather than dealing with a bank.

It was pretty interesting to watch because my broker was doing his best to get my low-doc loan over the line, and the real estate agent was calling my broker every day for an update on the status of my finance. And my broker found that pretty annoying, but obviously the agent was eager to close this deal.

Being new to property purchasing, I was hesitant about negotiating. Big mistake! When purchasing a property, you should never be scared to negotiate hard. Put up your hand and offer a good figure. I was lucky to get my first property at a pretty good price, but that owed more to the markets at the time than to my negotiating skills.

I bought that property without having any kind of strategy in place. I had no plan for creating a property portfolio at the time, but I knew it would become an investment, and I could always sell it to buy another property, or rent it out.

GOAL 2: MULTIPLE SOURCES OF INCOME

By the time I was 30 I had what I thought was a secure teaching job at an excellent school. I had a regular income and owned my own home — I was set, or so I thought.

Then, in 2007–2008, around about the time of global financial crisis, country after country around the globe was plunged into recession. A few people got laid off at my place of work, and I realised that, for most of us, job security is a bit of a myth. I thought, I really need to start investing.

I worked out that I needed to create multiple sources of income. I needed a vehicle that provided a good ongoing cashflow rather than relying on a job that might or might not exist in the uncertain future.

My Rockdale home didn't build much equity for the first few years, as I'd bought it at the wrong time in the cycle, just after the boom of the Sydney 2000 Olympic Games when Sydney property prices were in decline. So it hadn't increased a lot in value, but after three or four years it was at least heading in the right direction. And I realised that property was a good vehicle for me because it was less volatile than investments like shares.

LLOYD'S STRATEGY

You only need to save one deposit.

My advice these days is that to get started you really only need to save the deposit for your first property purchase. You can then buy subsequent properties using your equity in the first property by taking out a second loan — if you can satisfy the bank on your serviceability. But for me it wasn't a case of buy, increase the equity, buy the next one, rinse and repeat, the way I do these days. Back then I knew nothing about *manufacturing equity*.

So, because my first property wasn't enjoying much growth, when it came time to buy my next property, I had to rely on the money I'd continued to save to put down another deposit.

I didn't mind. I was always very comfortable putting my savings towards buying property. Even these days, I'm happy to save and put money into a property, knowing that such an investment will help me achieve greater financial freedom in the future. That Rockdale unit has now tripled in value, and I have actually refinanced it four times over the years to access the increased equity to help fund new purchases.

GOAL 3: PROPERTY UPGRADE AND FIRST INVESTMENT

When I started investing in property I hadn't even met Renee and I certainly wasn't thinking about paying for my future kids' education and owning a waterfront mansion, although I was teaching private-school kids who lived in those kinds of properties. What I did know was that in my current work situation I would never have a big income and wouldn't accrue much in the way of superannuation. I didn't want to spend my retirement living on a pension. I wanted financial freedom. These were the forces that drove me to taking investing seriously.

In 2007 I started looking at properties in the Campbelltown area of Sydney. I wanted to buy a bigger house to move into. My goal was to lease out Rockdale, and since it was brand new and well-located it did rent easily.

My new house would also later become an investment. This time I was leaving nothing to chance. I had a mate who lived out near the south-west suburb of Ingleburn and had bought his house there quite cheaply. That piqued my interest, because most areas in Sydney were already very expensive back then. So I looked around and found that I could afford a bigger property in Ingleburn.

After a little research I discovered that Ingleburn was experiencing a lot of capital growth and one of the lowest vacancy rates in the country, meaning that any property there should perform well over the longer term.

Eventually I found a three-bedroom villa at the end of a nice, quiet cul-de-sac, listed online through a real estate agent. I had looked at a few Ingleburn properties by then, but this one had a brand-new kitchen in it, which I loved (though I didn't even cook!). This house had a better kitchen than any house I'd ever lived in. So I made a very emotional purchase for about $262 000. I only had to put down a 10 per cent deposit, which was also a relief.

However, Ingleburn was 50 kilometres away from the Sydney CBD and from Bondi Junction, where I worked. It was on a train line, but my house was a long way from the station. I loved walking but it was a long walk to the shops if I had a lot of groceries to bring home, so I had to drive. I really enjoyed living in Ingleburn, though, because it was quiet and green and brought me back to my country roots.

I rode my motorbike to work when the weather allowed. I'd be up at 5 o'clock and out of the house at a quarter past, to make sure I missed most of the traffic, and I'd just fly down the side of the motorway in 45 minutes. I'd do the same in the dark on the way home, and that was my day. I met Renee while I was living there, and she'd climb on the back of the bike. It was great fun.

After we bought our home in Lewisham and moved in together, I kept that Ingleburn property as an investment for a few years, then sold it in

2012 — again at the wrong time in the market. I should have held onto it for a few more years. Had I sold it in 2021 I would have made heaps on it, as it would have more than doubled in value. Even if I'd kept it until 2018, I would have made a lot more. But you live and learn.

I wouldn't say it started to snowball from there, because although I was acquiring more properties, I still made some beginner's mistakes. This was mainly because I was still not clear on my goals and I didn't really have a strategy in place.

GOAL 4: STARTING A PROPERTY BUSINESS

After Renee and I got married we began to set some goals together — things like building up to a family, buying a dream home and creating a secure financial future. With that my successful investment strategies were formed at last. I'll tell you about those in chapter 6.

I had built up a cashflow-positive portfolio, and the rental income from my properties had actually replaced my teaching salary before I left the nine-to-five behind at age 40.

So I had a positively geared property portfolio that was paying me over $100 000 a year, and I had also set up my buyer's agency while I was still teaching. I had a lot going on — and three income streams.

At the time, growing my business along with my portfolio happened organically.

These days a lot of people ask me why I work as a buyer's agent and teach others about property when I have such a big property portfolio. Why don't I just retire and keep adding to my portfolio? But the reason for starting Aus Property Professionals was to help other people replicate my success and to show people how it can be done. I now employ a number of people in my business, so I am also creating jobs.

My *why* was to help other people see the bigger picture and create financial freedom through property. The best thing about what I do now is that I'm combining my two passions: teaching and property investment. Though I retired from a career as a schoolteacher, I still get to enjoy the element of teaching.

I feel very lucky that I have multiple sources of income, knowing that if something happens to my business, I'll always have the income from my property portfolio to fall back on. So I'm never stressed about money. I used to be. I know what it's like to have no money; I worked hard to put myself in a different position. That meant a lot of going without, working hard to save, setting a plan and believing in myself.

So I know it can work for you, because I've seen it work for me.

MY CURRENT GOALS

These days I'm content though still ambitious. I have a comfortable lifestyle. Another $10 million in the bank wouldn't necessarily change my current lifestyle, because I enjoy what I have. Sure, I'm going to keep investing and saving, but moving forward I want to just keep building security for my family, and I want my financial independence to continue.

So yes, I'm really, really happy with where I am in life and with where things are going. I've got two gorgeous young sons and a beautiful wife and love spending time with them. Certain goals have changed a bit since we started a family: putting the kids through school is part of our goal-setting these days.

When I'm buying investments now, things are different from when I started out in two very big ways. Firstly, I'm investing very much with Riley and Caelen in mind, knowing they will inherit those properties. Secondly, I don't have specific numbers in mind for how many dollars I want in the bank or how many more properties I want to acquire, because I'm already financially comfortable. At the moment, as well as continuing to invest, I'm also paying down debt, which we'll talk about in chapter 11.

I wasn't always so content. I lived in a shoebox of a one-bedroom apartment, then all the way out in Ingleburn. The next home we lived in was on a really busy road, and even though it was an expensive house in a good suburb, we had just one parking spot, so I let Renee park there while I'd park in another street — it was a nightmare.

These experiences drove my passion for that dream home on the water. But I couldn't just snap my fingers and buy it — I didn't have that kind of cash yet. I knew I had to work towards that — and I did.

FINDING YOUR MOTIVATION

I believe that money itself won't create happiness unless you already have the underlying seeds of happiness. If you're unhappy with something about yourself, having more money isn't likely to fix your problem. You have to own it and change it. For example, if you're unhappy about being physically unfit, then why not change it by signing up at the gym and getting seriously fit?

I have a morning routine that gets me up and feeling positive, so I get everything I can out of my day. I get Riley out of bed and get his breakfast sorted. He's always happy and cheeky in the morning.

I take my Boston Terrier Frankie for a run. Then I have to have a coffee — that's non-negotiable! I also like to sit and read the paper. That relaxes me and gets my head in the right space before I get into 'work mode'. Every evening I turn off email notifications on my phone. I have a rule that I don't check my phone after 8 pm, so I can spend uninterrupted time with my family.

These kinds of activities would make me happy whether or not I had money. It seems simple, but it's really important to find the motivation to keep doing the things in your life that create happiness. And if you have that nice lifestyle, money just adds to what you have created within yourself.

In my experience, you need a routine and to try to get everything you can from your life. Getting up early and going for a run might not work for everyone. You need to find your *own* routine and what you need to do to help you achieve *your* personal goals.

It's vital that you both believe in yourself and keep yourself accountable.

I believe it's important to have goals and to continue to set new ones, but you also need to recognise and reward yourself when you reach your current goals, to enjoy the satisfaction of your achievement and the knowledge that you're still moving forward.

Don't compare your performance with others' and try to keep up with other people. Think rather, 'Yes, I've achieved some good goals here and I'm happy about that.' I'm not suggesting you rest on your laurels, because I think we should always strive for something better. But equally, you shouldn't go through life thinking, I need more, I need to do better, but I'm never going to get there.

It's also very important that you believe in your dream, and in yourself, and keep working towards it while not being swayed by naysayers.

When I was still teaching, a lot of people told me, 'Investing is too risky—you're not going to make it.' Once I had four or five properties people said, 'Oh, don't buy any more—you'll go bankrupt!' But all the time I was educating myself and setting achievable goals. I knew my strategy was sound. I was confident I would be successful down the track because I knew I'd work hard until I got there. I backed myself.

CASE STUDY
THIS NEW INVESTOR'S GOALS CHANGED WHILE SHE WAS ON MATERNITY LEAVE

One client's story—of how while on maternity leave with her second child she took the reins of the family's financial planning—stands out for me.

Jane had a successful career, having worked her way up over 10 years in the corporate sector. She and her husband had been considering buying an investment property for a while and had been saving for a deposit for at least two years. But her savings were accumulating very slowly, on a low interest rate, and didn't reflect how hard she had worked and saved.

Frustrated, she knew she needed to find a way for her money to 'work smarter' for her. When she took maternity leave, with a newborn and a toddler to care for, Jane began to reflect on where she wanted her family to be financially in five, 10, even 20 years' time—and that was in a place of assured financial security.

But buying an investment property can be hard. Jane did some research on where to buy and what they could afford. She soon realised that budget limitations meant she'd have to purchase in another state. She wanted to ensure she did it right first time and didn't fall for any sales tactics or traps.

With a new baby, of course it was going to be difficult to do property inspections, especially for an investment property that wasn't close to where the family lived. So Jane employed Aus Property Professionals, and we helped her throughout the process.

Jane came to us with a budget of $450 000. I did a lot of the research and due diligence to ensure she bought in an area that was primed for growth. We chose one of the outer-ring suburbs of Brisbane for Jane's purchase. This was based on the planned infrastructure, which would fuel jobs growth in the area, and the population growth forecast for the suburb.

It was difficult to find properties in such a good area of a capital city that would be affordable, given Jane's budget. I searched both on and off market for something suitable. I considered but dismissed more than 10 properties, either because they were over budget or because they weren't 'investment-grade' properties. (I discuss what makes an investment-grade property in chapter 10.)

I finally sourced a newly built property with an asking price of $450 000, right on budget. As it was a new property, Jane would get maximum depreciation for tax purposes. I managed to negotiate a great price—$425 000, which was $25 000 under the asking price and below Jane's budget limit. This meant her rental yield was much

(continued)

higher than it would have been had we bought at the asking price, so she achieved better cashflow right away.

I ensured that the contracts were signed on the most favourable terms for her, including a 'subject to building and pest inspection' clause and a 60-day (rather than a 35-day) settlement period.

An excellent valuation of $540 000 just 12 months later demonstrated that we'd bought this property at the right time in the cycle, when the markets were beginning a growth phase.

Jane is now on the right path to building a positively geared property portfolio that will give her the freedom to make financial choices, such as working part-time so she can spend more time with her children, sending them to private schools and taking the family on an annual holiday.

THE NUMBERS

Property purchase price:	$425 000
Stamp duty:	$14 619
Legal costs:	$1550
Building and pest inspection:	$660
TOTAL PURCHASE COSTS:	**$441 829**
Rent per week:	$470
Yield:	5.75 per cent (excellent for a capital city)
Independent valuation results (12 months later):	$540 000
EQUITY GROWTH ACHIEVED IN THE FIRST 12 MONTHS:	**$98 171**

CHAPTER 2
YOUR FINANCIAL PLAN

Every property owner needs a brilliant budget

 After setting your short- and long-term goals, I recommend you set a financial goal to match them. If you're keen on getting a deposit together, getting a loan approved, paying off your home loans and achieving your goals fast, it's vital that you manage your money extremely well. That's why we're covering it first.

First I must state clearly that I'm not a financial adviser and any advice I give here is general in nature. Which is why, if you're starting from square one, you need to ask for help in managing your money from the financial experts in your dream team, such as your financial planner, mortgage broker and accountant. We'll look more closely at their roles in this chapter.

SETTING A FINANCIAL GOAL

All the strategies discussed in this book revolve around using the equity in one property as a deposit for the next, and building towards being able to comfortably buy your own home or to create a portfolio of positively geared properties that lead you to your dream home and/or financial freedom.

For instance, many clients come to me with the goal of attaining financial freedom through the strategy of setting up an annual passive income that clears $100 000. I explain to them that to do that, you actually need to be making more than $100 000, because you have to cover your expenses as a property owner.

You need a total annual rental income of around $175 000 to achieve $100 000 per year. This figure takes account of all the expenses you'll face, including rates and repairs on your properties and tax. To secure that amount each year, you'll need a $7 million portfolio, with either half of it paid off (so your mortgage repayments aren't eating up your cashflow) or the ability to sell down some of your properties to pay off all your debt, so you have an unencumbered portfolio of $3.5 million — that is, you need a $3.5 million rental property portfolio *paid off* to achieve that $100 000 income.

Perhaps you're looking for a strategy that will enable you to buy yourself a nice home, or even your dream home. For example, your financial goal may be to buy a $2 million home. We'll look at how best you might work up to that.

If you have saved a basic deposit of, say, $60 000, you would not be approved for a $2 million home loan, even if you have the income to support it. To finance that dream home, the strategy is still to *create enough equity* from investment properties to enable you to sell some of your properties to be approved for that loan.

Now, let's say you can obtain a mortgage for your dream home right now. Normally when you buy a property, you'll put down a 10 or 20 per cent deposit and take out an 80 or 90 per cent loan. But you wouldn't want to do this on a $2 million property: $1.8 million is a lot of debt, no matter what your means.

The key is to have enough savings to put down *at least half the price of the house*. Ideally, then, you'll put down a $1 million deposit and borrow the rest. A 50 per cent loan-to-value ratio (LVR) will put you in a great position when buying your dream home.

To be able to do that, you first need to build up your investments — through growth, both organic and manufactured, and through good cashflow. Then you can sell some of your properties when it's time to achieve that $2 million property goal. A time frame for that exit strategy is always important too, and I will go into that in chapter 11.

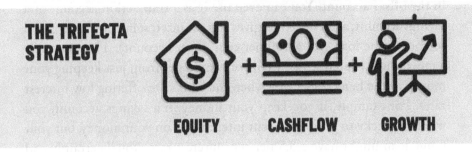

THE TRIFECTA STRATEGY

EQUITY + **CASHFLOW** + **GROWTH**

Put that first deposit down on one or more high-growth properties that offer good cashflow when rented; add equity to those properties to increase their immediate value; and refinance that higher value to buy more high-growth, good-cashflow properties.

HOW I PAID OFF MY HOUSES IN FIVE YEARS

Commonly people take out a 30-year home loan, paying it off out of their wages by making the basic minimum repayments. In fact, most people will never pay off their early homes. Instead, they'll sell, then start the 30-year mortgage again on their next home. But it doesn't have to be that way. Here are the main strategies I use to pay off my mortgages quickly.

1. I USE AN OFFSET ACCOUNT

An offset account acts like an everyday transaction account but has the benefit of saving you money on interest. The good thing about an offset account is that it is virtually the same as paying money directly into your loan, but you have more control over your money.

If your home loan is attached to an offset account, you can park any spare funds in that account, and you'll pay interest only on the difference between your mortgage balance and the balance in the offset account. For example, if you have a $100 000 mortgage and $10 000 in your offset account, interest is charged on only $90 000 ($100 000–$10 000) instead of on the entire balance.

The other major benefit is that you have full control over all the funds in the offset account. You can even use it as a transaction account or a savings account, as it effectively gives you the interest rate that is attached to your home loan (for a 100 per cent offset account). This is usually a much higher interest rate than you would get from just keeping your money in the bank, especially when the banks are offering low interest rates. For example, if you keep your money in a savings account, you would be lucky to get a 1 per cent interest rate on your money, but your home loan might have a 3.5 per cent interest rate. You'll certainly end up ahead this way.

The best way to use an offset account is to put all your savings into it. If you have an investment property, rental income can be paid into the offset account. It's where you should hold any spare cash you might have been able to access through refinancing equity from your home if it has increased in value.

Those savings can grow exponentially across the life of the loan, allowing you to pay off your 30-year mortgage over 20 years or even 10 years or less, depending on the size of the mortgage and how much you are contributing to the offset account. So that's a great way to pay off your property faster.

2. I USE MY EQUITY

When you first purchase a home, your equity is simply your deposit amount. Then, as you pay off your mortgage, any payment applied to the principal increases your equity in the property. Until you pay off your mortgage in full, your lender still has an interest in the property, although you're considered to be the owner.

Your equity also increases as your property's market value rises. You can manufacture additional equity by increasing the value of your home — for example, through renovations or development, which is what I'm all about.

For instance, if I were developing duplexes for the purpose of manufacturing equity, I would sell one half of the duplex and use the profit to pay down the home loan on my principal place of residence (PPOR). I might keep the other half of the duplex to rent out for cashflow, or I might sell both sides of the duplex and reinvest the profit.

If I sold a property for a profit of $100 000, I'd usually use all of that profit against my home loan. I'd put it into the offset account and take a big chunk off the interest on the property straight away. It would be there if I needed to take it back out to fund another investment property purchase, but while it was in the offset account it would be reducing the interest owing on my home loan.

I'll use a duplex I did in Fletcher, Newcastle, to illustrate this. The land cost $250 000 and the construction costs were $600 000. Once finished and subdivided, however, the units were valued by the bank at $550 000 each. So that development created $250 000 in equity. I decided to sell one of the units, and because the market was strong I was able to sell it for $570 000. Total debt on that side of the duplex was $425 000, so I made $145 000 in profit.

As I had sold after holding it for 12 months, I got a 50 per cent reduction on the capital gains tax (CGT), and I placed the profits left over in the Lewisham offset account to pay down some debt on that property. I kept the other side of the duplex and rented it out for a positive return. This was a process I repeated, not just with duplexes but with renovations, subdivisions and even land banking.

3. I MAKE MORE FREQUENT MORTGAGE PAYMENTS

Often people pay their mortgages each month. By paying fortnightly, as I do, you'll pay down more of the interest. There are 26 fortnights in a year, so if you pay fortnightly you're actually paying 13 months every year, so you pay down your interest faster. That extra month each year can take a few years off the duration of your loan.

Most banks have forms that require you to specify what payment frequency you prefer, and you might automatically tick 'monthly' because that's where your cashflow is, but if you tick that fortnightly box, you're actually going to save some interest. If you find it doesn't work for you, you can always ask your bank to change it.

Never treat anything as a 'set and forget'. You can also call your bank to renegotiate interest rates, something I'll talk more about in chapter 3.

4. I REFINANCE MY PROPERTIES

When you refinance, you pay out your current home loan by taking out a new one, either with your existing lender or through a different lender. Refinancing might make sense for you if your situation has changed — for example, if you have changed jobs or started a family.

You might also think about refinancing if the market conditions have changed – for example, if the refinancing involves replacing an existing loan with a new one that pays off the debt of the first one. Ideally, the new loan will offer a better interest rate and terms or features that improve your finances to make the whole process worthwhile.

Many times, rather than selling a property when preparing to buy another property, I'll just refinance it. When refinancing, though, I keep the money in my offset account so it is paying off my home loan in the meantime. Then, when I am ready to buy another property, I take out what money I need from the offset account. This way, I always put as much money as I can into the offset account to pay down the interest on that.

REFINANCING LIMITS

Yes, you can refinance equity, but only as much as your serviceability allows, and that depends on your income level, just as getting any mortgage does. If you're on a low income, you can't expect to be able to finance millions of dollars for your dream home through one loan. But you can refinance your existing loans and build up your portfolio. As the properties grow in value you can sell them in order to fund more expensive properties down the track. Refinancing your loans to banks offering lower interest rates can also help build up your equity and cashflow more quickly.

BUDGETING

I've already talked about the value of being frugal, and how it helped me stick to a budget in order to save. In the life of a property investor, budgeting is crucial every step of the way:

- You need to budget and save for your first deposit.
- The bank will need to see proof that you can budget and save before approving your home loan.
- You'll need to budget and manage money well to pay off your mortgages in less than 30 years.

When the time comes to apply for a loan, you need to demonstrate you are good with money. The trick to being frugal and sticking to a budget is knowing what you're spending your money on. Obviously, you need to save more than you're spending!

LLOYD'S SAVINGS TIP

Before you even begin looking at properties, it's wise to get a feel for the price brackets you'll be looking at and how much you'll need to save.

1. BE REALISTIC ABOUT WHERE TO START YOUR PROPERTY SEARCH

It's smart to think long and hard about where you should start, rather than where you hope to end up.

2. DEVELOP GOOD SAVING HABITS EARLY

Track all of your purchases to identify areas where you overspend.

- Cut back on:
  - big-ticket items
  - holidays

- takeaway coffee and meals
- Pay TV subscriptions — you don't need Netflix, Stan *and* Foxtel!
- pricey clothes and designer sunnies.

- Spend less than you earn and use the difference to pay down debt, save and invest.

- Pay off credit cards, loans and hire purchase agreements.

- Create a savings plan (for example, save 15 per cent of your income in a separate account).

- Open a high-interest account to put savings into, and set up regular deposits.

3. SAVE MORE BY PRETENDING YOU ALREADY OWN A HOME

Plan your finances as if you already have a home, as mortgage payments could be significantly higher than your rent and owning a home can come with a whole lot of extra costs, from council rates to maintenance fees. This will help you identify the things you are actually willing to sacrifice, as opposed to what you believe (hypothetically) you can live without. It's also a great way to start setting more money aside for your deposit.

MY FRUGAL PHILOSOPHY

Of course, most people want to live life and enjoy it now, and not to feel like getting ahead is difficult and painful and involves lots of sacrifices. If you save and budget well, you should be able to treat yourself to a nice dinner out once a month, or get coffee or breakfast out on the weekend, but not during the week. Renee and I like to buy takeaways on Friday nights to celebrate a good week.

I never bought a new car and didn't have a credit card until I had a considerable property portfolio and was on my way to financial independence. I never even took an overseas holiday until I was about 30. I'm still frugal when I buy clothes. I'll go and buy a cheap T-shirt rather than spending hundreds of dollars on designer items.

Call me old-school but when I see young people with a bit of money spend $300 on a pair of sunglasses, I can't help thinking, why don't you just buy a pair for $40 and save the difference? Every time you're tempted to buy something from a designer brand, why not look for a cheaper version and save the difference. You'll be able to save much more quickly.

TRACK YOUR SPENDING PATTERNS

Watching what you spend will actually help you get a mortgage. Banks now look closely at customers' bank statements to ascertain their living expenses and draw a picture of their spending patterns. Lenders will always check how much money you spend on eating out and takeaways. If you can show that you're more frugal and spend less than most people, that will help you get a home loan. What banks like to see in your bank statements is *a pattern of savings*. They want to see that at least *5 per cent* of your deposit is genuine savings. This is why I always recommend to my clients that they keep their bank statements fairly clean.

These days people often don' t track how much they're spending. I see this regularly. They think they're spending $3000 a month when they're actually spending $4000 or even $5000.

WHAT LENDERS LOOK FOR WHEN ASSESSING YOUR APPLICATION

Ultimately lenders want to be confident that you're a good candidate for a loan with the capacity to pay it off.

» Extra cash, whether from a tax return or a cash gift from your parents, that contributes to your deposit won't show that you're a good saver; you must demonstrate positive spending habits as well.

» Lenders will also look at in-store credit and instalment plans. If you're using these now, lenders will assume you'll continue to use them after you take out a home loan.

(continued)

> » When it comes to credit cards, it's all about the limit, not the balance. Even if your balance stands at $0, having a limit of $10 000 is viewed as your having $10 000 in accessible credit. If you can do without a credit card, cancel it.

WHERE TO START?

The best advice I can give to first-time investors is to draw up a budget. This might sound boring, but it's definitely the best way to set yourself up properly.

LLOYD'S STRATEGY

If you're keen to start using my tried-and-tested budget planner to keep track of your incomings and outgoings, it's right here.

Understand where your money is going. From there you can work backwards to see what you really need to start cutting back on. Normally I recommend a three- to four-month process, during which you examine your bank statements every month to determine whether you're moving towards your spending goals. It's worth tightening your belt for those few months, as the rewards you can gain from a good property portfolio far outweigh the frustrations of a few months of forgone extravagance.

Government grants are continually changing, but even without a grant, if you were to receive some money as a gift or a loan from your parents or family, the banks will accept that as savings as long as they can also see at least 5 per cent in genuine savings through your bank transactions.

YOUR FINANCE TEAM

Now to the key financial players on your dream team. If you can enlist the same buyer's agent, solicitor, mortgage broker and accountant across every property in your portfolio, they can work together to support your interests and provide consistent advice. Even now I ask my accountant for advice all the time, as well as consulting my solicitor or my broker.

MORTGAGE BROKER

HOW MUCH DOES A MORTGAGE BROKER COST?

Mortgage brokers won't cost you anything, as they are paid by the banks. Some do charge an upfront fee of around $500 to start the process, though this should be returned if you proceed with the loan they help you with. But most do not charge at all.

HOW DO I FIND ONE?

They can be found via an online Google search or on the Mortgage and Finance Association of Australia (MFAA) website (mfaa.com.au). Check that any broker you work with is an MFAA member and has the appropriate financial services licence.

WHAT DO THEY DO?

A mortgage broker acts as an intermediary between borrowers looking for home loans and lenders offering those loans.

Mortgage brokers may have access to 30 or more different lenders. They can offer personalised advice to help you choose the right home loan for your needs. This will often result in a better fit than if you go straight to a bank and are offered only one loan from that bank.

In Australia, every mortgage broker is required by law to carry an Australian Credit Licence (ACL) if offering credit assistance services. They must also comply with the regulations laid down by the Australian Securities and Investments Commission (ASIC). These regulations, as stipulated by Australian legislation, require mortgage brokers to comply with what are called 'responsible lending' and 'best interest' obligations.

Responsible lending obligations require brokers to suggest 'suitable' home loans. This means loans for which you easily qualify, loans that actually meet your needs and won't prove unnecessarily challenging for you.

👥 SOLICITOR/CONVEYANCER

HOW MUCH DOES A SOLICITOR OR CONVEYANCER COST?

Fees for both range from $1500 to $3000; $1800 is fairly average, but they may charge more for extra searches in relation to the property.

HOW DO I FIND ONE?

Online is a good place to start. You can also ask for recommendations from your buyer's agent, mortgage broker or accountant. Solicitors and conveyancers need to be licensed to practise in the state you're buying in.

WHAT DO THEY DO?

Solicitors and conveyancers complete and lodge all relevant documents and search the Certificate of Title via the relevant government body in each state.

Your solicitor or conveyancer will also search government department files and consult local authorities for anything that might affect the property, such as encumbrances or caveats, and make the necessary enquiries about zoning, titles and council and water rates. They can adjust rates and taxes, and liaise with the seller's conveyancer regarding settlement.

A solicitor or conveyancer will also ensure that all special conditions in the contract are fulfilled before settlement takes place, and will liaise with financial institutions on your behalf regarding the funds required to proceed to settlement.

Finally, they will prepare the settlement statement and attend settlement on your behalf.

👥 ACCOUNTANT

HOW MUCH DOES AN ACCOUNTANT COST?

The cost will depend on the scope of the work required. Tax returns might cost $150 whereas setting up a trust can cost $1500, so it depends on your requirements.

HOW DO I FIND ONE?

Ask other professionals on your dream team for recommendations.

WHAT DO THEY DO?

I highly recommend you get a good accountant on your team. Whether you're buying or selling property, you should always seek professional advice from your accountant early in the process.

There are a few important things you need your accountant to do for you.

1. They need to know your long-term investment strategy

Your accountant needs to adopt a holistic approach and seek to understand what you're trying to achieve financially and where you want to be over the long term.

Your accountant can advise you on the best structure for you as an individual purchaser of property to use when buying the property — that is, whether the property should be purchased in a trust, in a company structure or in your own name. An accountant can also advise you on the tax implications of each entity, asset protection and the best tax minimisation strategy for your needs.

Your accountant also needs to ensure you're getting the best possible return from your property. They must understand everything you can claim on your property. There's a lot more to their role than just doing a tax return claiming interest and depreciation.

2. They must be experienced in property

A property accountant works in the real estate industry to help individuals, companies and developers with budget analysis, audit reporting, portfolios, reconciliation and more.

Property accountants prepare, maintain and review financial records, commercial property agreements and residential property agreements, as well as dealing with some rentals.

3. They must be available

It's important to keep the lines of communication open with your accountant, so if the right property pops up, you know your numbers and can act quickly. You need to be able to ask your accountant immediately, 'Can I do this? What are the ramifications?'

Today I have the same team around me that I recommend to my clients, and I still ask my accountant questions even if I think I know the answers. It's vital that I know exactly what I'm doing before I get into my next deal.

If you're trying to handle everything yourself at tax time, it's information overload! A good accountant can help you get your head around things like property spreadsheets and financial statements from your property managers.

4. They should advise you on ownership structures and entities

Your accountant can also help you determine the best ownership structure for your investment properties, for asset protection and for tax purposes. For example, you might buy one property in your own name, but if you're buying several properties, setting yourself up with trust structures will be important.

When I first started investing, I was buying properties in my own name. Later I began to think more about the bigger picture. I wanted to be able to buy properties for my kids, to pass them down and distribute income through discretionary trusts. So I started setting up trusts.

It's crucial to get that advice from your accountant upfront, *before* you buy the property, rather than when you're in the middle of exchanging contracts on a property, or when you've already gone unconditional on the property and you suddenly think, oh, actually I don't want to buy it in my name, I want to buy it in a trust.

It's way too late by that stage, because setting up a trust can take a few days. You should also be aware that it can be expensive to buy a property in one entity, then change entities later, because to do so you'll need to pay a second lot of stamp duty.

OWNERSHIP STRUCTURES

There are five basic ownership structures:

Individual: You buy a property in your own name, as most people do when they purchase their primary place of residence (PPOR). The advantage of this structure is it allows you to sell your property later and not pay capital gains tax (CGT) on the profits, and you can also access a 50 per cent discount on CGT if you've held the property for at least 12 months as an investor before reselling.

Partnership: A partnership involves two or more individuals and operates in a similar fashion to buying a property individually.

Company: A company structure is useful if you want to limit your personal liability; however, you will have to pay tax at the company rate of 30 per cent. This structure is often suited to small developments, particularly if there are multiple people involved. Companies do not qualify for a 50 per cent exemption on CGT.

Trust: Trusts can be a great tool for property investors as they enable them to access the 50 per cent CGT discount. There are two main types of trust: unit trusts and discretionary trusts. Unit trusts have a structure similar to that of a company, with fixed units allocated to individual investors. Discretionary trusts have no fixed entitlements, and distributions are made at the discretion of the trustee.

Self-managed super fund (SMSF): Is a variation of a trust structure. Generally, you need at least $200 000 to set up an SMSF, and they are not suited to small developments and subdivisions. Borrowing for an SMSF can also be difficult at times.

KEEP YOUR RECORDS STRAIGHT

Make sure you've got all your records, and give them to your accountant to keep on file. For example, I get my tax done by an accountant, which means I don't need to have it done by 31 October — I can get it done by May the following year.

But when my statements from my real estate agents, and everything else relating to my tax, come in at the end of each financial year, I send them straight to my accountant. This means that when my accountant does my tax the following year, it's all on record there. That way, even if you're a bit disorganised, it'll still all be on file, so it's harder for the accountant to mess up or for you to leave money on the table.

BUYING IN DIFFERENT STATES

Once you own enough properties in one state to have reached the land tax threshold, you will need to start paying land tax. If you buy in a different state next time, you begin at $0, until you reach that state's land tax threshold. To minimise the land tax you'll have to pay, it's good to buy in different states and territories as well as using different entities, such as trusts.

In 2021 the NSW Government proposed the option of either paying a one-off stamp duty of 4 per cent up front or paying land tax annually. Land tax is like council rates, reducing your income on an investment property.

Stamp duty is a disincentive to selling your house in order to upsize or downsize. The transaction fees in selling one house and buying another can be in the hundreds of thousands. At this stage, though, stamp duty still looks more appealing than land tax, as land tax rates can be very high.

Buying in different structures can help. If you buy some properties in your own name and some in a trust, then you're buying in different entities and will have a separate land tax threshold for each entity. Overall you'll have a higher land tax threshold and can therefore buy more properties in each state or territory.

Remember that I'm not offering financial or tax advice. Be sure to speak with your accountant before you decide.

LAND TAX IN AUSTRALIA

» **NSW:** revenue.nsw.gov.au/taxes-duties-levies-royalties/land-tax

» **VIC:** sro.vic.gov.au/land-tax

» **QLD:** qld.gov.au/environment/land/tax

» **SA:** revenuesa.sa.gov.au/landtax

» **WA:** wa.gov.au/organisation/department-of-finance/land-tax

» **ACT:** revenue.act.gov.au/land-tax

» **TAS:** sro.tas.gov.au/land-tax

» **NT:** The Northern Territory does not charge land tax

NEGATIVE VS POSITIVE GEARING

Your rental property is 'positively geared' if your deductible expenses are less than the income you earn from the property — that is, if you make a profit from renting out your property. Your rental property is 'negatively geared' if your deductible expenses are more than the income you earn from the property.

I'm not a fan of negative gearing; however, for tax purposes, even positively geared properties have negative-gearing benefits.

Because the overall tax result of a negatively geared property is a net rental loss, you may be able to claim a deduction for the full amount of your rental expenses against your rental and *other* income, such as salary, wages or business income. If your other income is insufficient to absorb the loss, you can carry forward your loss to the next income year.

This is why having the ability to negatively gear properties can be quite attractive. It was never designed to help multimillionaires who have lots of properties in their portfolio, but it is beneficial to 'mum-and-dad investors' who are trying to get ahead.

BUYING PROPERTY WHEN YOU'RE SELF-EMPLOYED

Forward planning is critical when you're self-employed; otherwise, it can be difficult to invest in property.

If you've made plans with your mortgage broker to borrow funds to buy a home or build wealth — or borrow money for any other purpose — your broker's objective is to make you look like a financially viable prospect for the banks. Remember: banks typically base how much they are prepared to lend on your income and expenses.

However, while you want to present potential lenders with evidence of a high income in order to be able to borrow as much as possible, your accountant is trying to minimise that same income for tax reasons. This is why it's important that you introduce your broker to your accountant. That way, they can put their heads together to work out the best strategy for your situation.

BUYING PROPERTY WITH A SELF-MANAGED SUPER FUND (SMSF)

Sometimes buying property within an SMSF is a good way to go, such as when you have a lot of money in super. Generally, you can't consider buying a property via a super fund unless you have at least $200 000 in it. But there are certainly some good options if you do.

There are a few rules around buying in an SMSF. For example, you can't buy a property inside the SMSF and then subdivide it, as an SMSF purchase needs to be made on a single contract. If you buy some land and then build, that involves two contracts (land + construction). If you want to build or subdivide, you'll need to purchase the land in some other entity, such as a trust, or even in individual names.

I suggest setting up an SMSF when you buy a property, as part of a long-term strategy. Perhaps you buy something in a higher growth area with good cashflow that's going to pay off the property. I've definitely had clients use their super in positive ways to get into those blue-chip suburbs that are sure to do well.

Buy property outside of your super fund too, so you've got two vehicles running at the same time.

The fees are fairly transparent in a SMSF in comparison with those in an industry fund. Setting up an SMSF costs about $1000, and you pay an annual supervisory levy of around $249 to the Australian Taxation Office (ATO). There are also accounting fees and your fund must be audited annually by an asset auditor, typically for a fee of $1000 or upwards.

FIVE TIPS FOR PROPERTY INVESTORS AT TAX TIME

Australia has very generous tax deductions for property investors. The ATO reports that around 8 per cent of Australians own an investment property, and it treats those investments like businesses. That means your investment expenses can be claimed as tax deductions, helping you to minimise your income tax bill.

Some years the ATO cracks down on certain things, including rentals, holiday and investment properties, and other vehicles. Excessive expenses claims, and incorrectly appointed rental income and expenses then come under the microscope. So it's important to be equipped with the right information and tools.

1. KEEP RECORDS OF EVERYTHING

If you invest in a rental property, you'll need to keep records right from the start. You'll need these records to calculate expenses that can be claimed as deductions, and to ensure you declare all rental income in your tax return. If you're claiming expenses related to items you've purchased for the property, you'll need receipts for those.

Your tax accountant will be across all the finer details. Your property manager also plays an important role at tax time and should have provided you with all the relevant documents for your property. An end-of-financial-year (EOFY) statement should detail items such as total rental income for the year, total fees paid to the managing agent, and out-of-pocket expenses such as council rates, water rates and any maintenance work done on the property.

2. COMPLETE PROPERTY MAINTENANCE BEFORE EACH EOFY

Any necessary maintenance work or repairs you carry out before the end of the fiscal year are expenses you can claim sooner. If you miss the 30 June EOFY deadline, you'll have to wait another 12 months to claim these costs.

3. DECLARE ALL YOUR RENTAL INCOME – INCLUDING RENTAL BONDS

Property investors need to declare all the income generated from their property in the financial year. This includes not just rental income, but also any rental bond money you are entitled to retain — for example, when a tenant defaults on rent or you incur maintenance costs, and receive insurance payouts as a result.

4. WORK OUT EXACTLY WHAT YOU CAN AND CAN'T CLAIM

Many things, from council rates and landlord insurance to loan setup fees, can be claimed as rental-related expenses. Investors can claim the costs of repairs and maintenance, loan interest charges and fees, legal expenses, and decline in value of depreciable assets in the property, such as carpets, curtains and dishwashers.

Claim as much as you can — don't miss a thing. Not claiming enough or the right expenses can cost property owners hundreds or even thousands of dollars on their tax returns.

For more information on what you can and cannot claim at tax time, visit ato.gov.au.

5. UNDERSTAND HOW DEPRECIATION CAN WORK FOR YOU

Depreciation is another key area commonly overlooked by novice property investors. A depreciation schedule is a report that outlines the decline in value of certain assets within a property, such as carpets, appliances, plant and equipment.

Property owners can claim depreciation on wear and tear of these assets. This depreciation can be claimed in your tax return each financial year, and can save you thousands of dollars.

Appoint a qualified quantity surveyor to produce a depreciation schedule for each property you buy. When I first started I didn't even know what a depreciation schedule was. A few years down the track, I had to backtrack and get it done for the first couple of properties I'd bought. Then I realised I could do them for every property. You can claim depreciation over a period of up to 40 years.

As my portfolio grew, I made sure I was getting those reports all the time, especially for duplex developments. You can get really good depreciation on those, because you've essentially got two of everything.

That said, I don't advocate buying an investment property or building a property just because you want to claim depreciation! Tax deductions are one positive outcome, not an investment strategy or reason to invest. But if you're leaving money on the table, you're disadvantaging yourself.

You can get better returns on newer properties, which typically need less maintenance. It's important to think about that when investing.

CASE STUDY
$100K EQUITY WITHIN SIX MONTHS ON A $300K PURCHASE

Michael and Liz had worked hard over the years to save a deposit to get their foot in the door of property investing, but they had no idea where to start. Unsure of what strategy would help them achieve their goals, they reached out to me for guidance.

THE STRATEGY

I sat down with them to explore their options and determine the best strategy moving forward. We looked at their current financial position and where they wanted to be in five, 10 and 15 years' time.

As parents, they wanted to set themselves up financially so they could spend more time with their kids and not have to worry about their business all day and night. After reading some of our clients' success stories, they loved the idea of building a duplex, but with bank financing of just under $350k, they didn't yet have a big enough deposit to be able to do this.

We decided that buying a house on a large block of land with subdivision potential was going to provide the best returns for them. To do this within budget meant that we had to look into regional towns, where there was still good potential for growth as well as the opportunity to manufacture instant equity.

We wanted to be able to keep the original house on the block and rent it out while the subdivision process took place, with the potential to build a duplex on the new lot when they had the funds to do so. This meant they would be earning an income on their investment from day one, while also being able to manufacture equity on their newly created subdivided block down the track.

THE CHALLENGES

With large blocks of land becoming scarcer in top-performing regional towns, we had to dig deep to find the right property.

Most importantly, we needed to ensure that Michael and Liz would be permitted to build a duplex on the new lot. As usual, we spoke with the council, town planners, draftspeople and builders to ensure that a subdivision and duplex build could proceed.

ACQUISITION

We narrowed our search area to a town in NSW with excellent performance, where we'd had great success over the years with other clients. After shortlisting and inspecting a number of properties, we found a house that ticked all the boxes: a solid, three-bedroom, brick-veneer home on a 1618 sq m block. It was well within budget, located close to amenities and had the layout we needed to do a subdivision.

It had an asking price of $335k, which already represented good value, but we were able to negotiate $35k off the asking price and secure the property for $300 000. Michael and Liz were thrilled to learn that the tenants already living in the property and paying rent of $330 per week were happy to stay on, ensuring their mortgage repayments would be covered.

THE RESULTS

After settling on the property, Michael and Liz decided to pursue the strategy of subdividing. With the assistance of a local surveyor we'd dealt with many times, the subdivision approvals process went smoothly.

Once the subdivision was completed, it was time to ask the bank to value the original house plus the new vacant lot and find out what the two individual properties were now worth.

(continued)

THE NUMBERS

Property purchase price:	$300 000
Stamp duty:	$9259
Subdivision costs (mostly paid to council and to the surveyor for carrying out the work and preparing the subdivision documentation):	$30 000
TOTAL PURCHASE COSTS:	**$339 259**
Independent valuation results:	
Main house (on smaller block):	$285 000
Newly created block:	$155 000
TOTAL VALUE:	**$440 000**
TOTAL INSTANT EQUITY MANUFACTURED AFTER COSTS:	**$100 741**

Note: No legal fees were paid as purchasers used a family friend (who is a conveyancer).

Michael and Liz were extremely happy with the result. We'd helped them to manufacture $100 741 in equity on a $300k purchase, all within six months. They're now getting ready to use this money as the deposit for building a duplex on their newly created lot. This means they don't have to find and buy a vacant lot, eliminating the need to pay stamp duty again (which means even more money in their pockets).

On completion of their duplex, they'll be manufacturing even more equity, which will set them up to invest in a second property and achieve their goals much faster than your average 'buy and hold' investor.

CHAPTER 3

GET THAT MORTGAGE

The ins and outs of getting financing approved first go

 From buying an investment property to building a property portfolio to buying a dream home to becoming financially free—all my strategies involve building wealth through borrowing money. This chapter covers the nuts and bolts of working with a mortgage broker and some of the money management and lifestyle factors that affect buying one or more properties.

Arguably the most powerful component of property investing is the investor's ability to borrow a large portion of a property's value from the bank.

Effectively, you're using other people's money (that is, money the bank has borrowed from other people through paying them interest) to build your own wealth. In many cases, you can borrow 90 per cent or more from a lender, which means you can control a large property portfolio after having fronted up with a relatively small amount of cash. This is at the heart of how I have built my own property portfolio.

No lender would allow you to borrow 90 per cent to invest in shares or any other asset class. This is why property investing is such an incredible way for most Australians on average incomes to build wealth.

To put it in context, you can buy a $500 000 property with only a $50 000 deposit (plus closing costs, such as stamp duty and legal fees). If that property increases in value by just 10 per cent, you've effectively just doubled your money. That's the power of leverage in property investment.

At the time of writing, the standard mortgage in most urban areas of Sydney is around a hefty $800 000. To put down a 20 per cent deposit, you're probably going to have to save a couple of hundred grand to cover the deposit and closing costs — and then you'll have an $800 000 mortgage.

However, until you know what kind of money the bank says you can borrow, you won't know what you're able to take on, which means you can't form a strategy. You can't do anything before talking to the banks — or, better, to a mortgage broker.

GETTING PRE-APPROVAL

So your property purchasing journey starts with your getting a clear understanding of how much money you're able to borrow from a bank. To do this you need to speak with your mortgage broker about getting pre-approval (conditional approval) for a home loan.

Pre-approvals are given based on your income and debt levels and how the bank sees your serviceability.

Typically, your mortgage broker will collect from you all the documents a lender will require, including ID, payslips, tax returns and bank statements, including those relating to any other loans that you may have. Your broker will then assess your personal circumstances, using that information to find the loan product from their panel of lenders that will best suit your needs.

Mortgage brokers do all the loan analysis legwork for you. They generally have close working relationships with a range of lenders and will be able to get a clear indication up front as to whether you're likely to get finance. If it appears likely that the loan will be approved, a mortgage broker can prepare the paperwork for you to sign and advise you when they receive confirmation that you have been pre-approved.

You need to collect all the relevant documents, ready to give to the bank for pre-approval. When you have found the property you want to buy, you pass the Contract of Sale for that property to the bank, so they can do a valuation and approve your loan.

LENDER VALUATIONS

The bank must value the property independently, because that property becomes their security in exchange for loaning you the money. The bank's valuation represents what they could sell that property for to get their money back in the event that you, the buyer, default.

For example, if you buy a property for $500000, the bank might need to sell it for only $450000 because they have a $450000 loan on it. The bank will appoint an independent valuer who will do a market appraisal of the property using comparable sales as a benchmark. The bank needs to check that the purchase price is in line with what the valuer views as the market value of the property.

Bank valuations don't always correspond to market value. Sometimes they come in short, particularly in a hot market. So you need to understand what the markets are doing to appreciate whether the property you're planning to buy is reasonably priced or overpriced. I'll return to this in later chapters.

If you've just made an offer on a property and the bank's valuer assesses that property's value at less than you're paying for it, you may have to come up with *more* money to get your loan approved. For example, if you offer $1 million for a property in a hot market, and a bank valuation is $900000, the lender will only lend you the loan-to-value ratio up to $900000 to buy that property; that is, the bank will lend you either 80 or 90 per cent of $900000, not of the $1 million purchase price. You'll have to come up with the shortfall, which in this instance would be $100000 on top of your deposit and purchase costs.

If a valuation comes in low, I always order a second one. If that valuation also comes in low, I use it to try to negotiate a lower purchase price if we are still in the cooling-off or finance approval period. Perhaps the valuer has not used the most recent comparables or, in a hot market, kept up with market increases — all this can be taken into account.

GETTING IN EARLY

You need to be ready to buy as soon as a property is available. Some banks can take two or three weeks to approve loans, even when you already have pre-approval. If you don't have pre-approval, the lead time to get pre-approval in place can be in excess of four to six weeks, depending on the bank, the current market and the buyer's circumstances.

People say, 'That's okay. My broker said we can just bring them the contract once we've got the property'. But it doesn't work like that, because if you haven't yet even given the broker your financials, the property will likely have sold by the time you get a loan approved.

To mitigate that risk, I have a policy of ensuring my clients' finance is always pre-approved, with the loans in place before we go shopping for property. As well as giving them the best chance of securing a property, this helps us to build strong relationships with the selling agents too, as they know that my buyer's agency always comes to them with qualified buyers.

WORKING WITH A MORTGAGE BROKER OVER THE LONG TERM

The job of a good mortgage broker is not simply to help get you a loan. A mortgage broker plays a key role in helping you build wealth through property, because you'll need a different mortgage for every property you acquire.

Your broker should be looking at the big picture, helping you plan how to acquire not just one property, but multiple properties down the track, and to make that work as well as it can using the various investment strategies available to you.

Your broker will model your borrowing capacity. Your strategy depends on serviceability and the factors that influence how banks assess potential clients. Typically, lenders will let you borrow only a certain amount of money, based on your personal income and expenses, as well as the prospective income (rent) from the property you're looking to purchase and any other properties you might own.

If you already have an investment property, your broker will calculate your borrowing capacity based on the property you already own, plus any future borrowings you want to make. Only then will they determine whether you can borrow to buy another property.

GETTING THE BEST POSSIBLE LOAN

Typically, when people go to a bank seeking a property loan, they're offered just one solution. A mortgage broker may have 30 or more different lenders on their books. Which lender your mortgage broker recommends will depend on your specific circumstances. A good broker will usually recommend three solutions to you, from three different lenders, and explain the differences between these loans and how each of them would work for you.

It has become more difficult to access loans in today's tough environment. Since the Australian Prudential Regulation Authority (APRA) got involved during the property boom of 2016–18, and off the back of the Banking Royal Commission, lending has become much more rigid, and it can be difficult to access funds in 2019.

A good mortgage broker monitors the various banks' policies and calculation loopholes closely. Bank policies do change regularly, so make sure the broker you choose is on top of that.

Before you sign up with a lender, look carefully at the overall loan package and educate yourself. That's the best advice I can give you. Ask your mortgage broker to help you understand what you're signing.

STRUGGLING WITH SERVICEABILITY

My clients often struggle with loan serviceability, which restricts them to a certain class of investment. If you're facing income instability because your business has closed down or you have lost your job, that presents a hurdle — but it doesn't mean you can't get a loan or refinance.

Depending on your circumstances, a mortgage broker may help you find finance through a non-bank lender. At the very least, they can show you what you need to do to satisfy the bank's criteria.

For example, if you have been knocked back by a major lender such as Commonwealth Bank of Australia or National Australia Bank, a broker can usually find a solution through a non-bank lender such as Pepper Money or Liberty.

I myself have three loans with Pepper, all of them set up for me by brokers. These lenders are really useful for people who are on lower incomes or are self-employed, or those who have a lot of properties, and are having problems around serviceability.

BORROWING CAPACITY FORMULA

Gross income − tax − existing commitments − new commitments − living expenses − buffer = monthly surplus

This example of one month's spending should 'pass' the lender's serviceability calculator:

Income:	$10 000
Tax:	$2000
Existing credit card payments:	$500
New home loan repayments:	$3000
Living expenses:	$2000
Buffer:	$500
Surplus:	$2000 per month

IMPROVING YOUR SERVICEABILITY

Serviceability requirements have definitely changed over the past few years. To determine your serviceability, your mortgage broker has to look at the full picture of your finances. When working with a mortgage broker, it's important to understand ways you can help improve both the odds of getting your loans approved and how much a bank will lend you. It's also useful to understand some of the key decisions you'll need to make around loan features.

Here are some tips to *boost your serviceability* from one of my own mortgage brokers, Jerone Balagtas:

 Reduce any ongoing expenses, such as subscriptions and memberships, in the months leading up to applying for a home loan.

 Consolidate and pay off any high-interest debts that are adding to your monthly expenses.

 Improve your credit score by paying bills the day you receive them and never paying them late. Your credit score reflects how you manage debt, and lenders will set an interest rate based on how much risk you pose to them.

Get rid of any credit cards you don't need. Lenders take into consideration your entire available credit, not just how much you currently owe. So if you have a credit card with a $10 000 limit, the lender will assume this is maxed out and will reduce your loan serviceability accordingly, even if you don't owe anything on the card.

As discussed in chapter 2, the banks like to see savings and a clean transaction account. For first home buyers who are saving for a deposit, it's a good idea to have two separate bank accounts: one for everyday spending and one for savings.

If you can, put at least 15 per cent of your earnings into a savings account; look for one that earns some interest. Ensure you don't have a credit card attached to your new savings account, so you're not tempted to use it. Even if it comes with a debit card, leave that at home so you never spend from that account. Use the savings account only when you need to transfer money to pay the deposit on a property. It could also be used as an emergency fund account or buffer.

If you currently own property, the best way to save is to put any extra money you can into the offset account of that property. Offsetting the interest against a property will net you higher interest than you'd get by leaving it in a savings account.

RAISING A DEPOSIT: DON'T MAX YOURSELF OUT

LLOYD'S STRATEGY

One question I'm frequently asked is, 'When's the best time to buy or start investing in property?' My answer is always the same: 'The best time to buy is when you *can* buy.'

When raising a deposit, you must ensure you're not overcommitting yourself. Don't think you need to maximise your borrowing power right away.

When I was embarking on my first and second property purchases I didn't have much in the way of deposits. My main focus was trying to find lower-priced properties, like that small apartment in Rockdale and the house in the outer suburb of Ingleburn. The banks were happy to lend me a bit more at the time, but I always wanted to borrow a bit *less* than they offered, because that would increase my borrowing power next time.

Borrowing less than your limit means you'll pay less of a deposit and less stamp duty. If you're borrowing more than 80 per cent of the property's value, you'll have to pay Lenders Mortgage Insurance (LMI), but the less you borrow, the less relative LMI you'll pay. All those savings help you. And if you're risk adverse, you'll be pleased to know that all those incremental savings minimise your financial risk too.

USING LENDERS MORTGAGE INSURANCE (LMI) TO MAXIMISE YOUR DEPOSIT

LMI is an insurance premium put in place to protect the lender in the event the borrower is unable to repay the loan. Normally you are required to pay LMI when the loan-to-value ratio on the property you're looking to purchase is greater than 80 per cent.

If you pay LMI, you're allowed to borrow up to 90 per cent or even more against the property. The net result is that you've got more money, using less deposit, to be able to buy an investment property. You're effectively increasing your leverage and using OPM (other people's money).

Some property purchasers hesitate to pay LMI, but there are advantages to being able to put down a smaller deposit.

I always think, if you've got enough deposit to buy a property for 20 per cent deposit, why not buy two properties at 10 per cent each? If you buy two properties, you can then turn those into four properties, and so on.

In practice, if you've got a $140 000 deposit, instead of buying one $500 000 property with an 80 per cent loan, you could pay the LMI premium and then, provided you can service the loan, buy two $500 000 properties, each with a 90 per cent loan (plus closing costs).

If you have only a small deposit, consider paying the LMI and getting into the market sooner. If you wait until you've saved a larger deposit, the markets may move on, leaving you behind. This has certainly been the case over the past 10 years as property values have steadily risen in many areas along Australia's east coast.

I grew my portfolio using LMI, so don't be scared of paying it or be put off by people who suggest it's a waste of money. If LMI helps you get ahead, that's really important. Of course, it still depends on your circumstances and whether the bank will lend you up to 90 per cent.

It's good to use a tool like LMI to get started, but over the longer term, as your portfolio grows, you'll also have to consider cashflow, because you don't want to overextend yourself. It's important to remember that if you are borrowing 90 per cent of the property's value, you'll have to be able to handle the repayments. That will be even more important if interest rates rise and you own multiple properties.

If you're buying your own home, I recommend you pay a 20 per cent deposit on it if you can. You cannot claim LMI on a home purchase, however, as it's not tax deductible. LMI can be claimed as a capitalised expense on your investment property. That is, you can claim it when you sell the property in the future.

CREDIT CARDS AND REWARDS

Be aware of the 'honeymoon periods' and special deals with which the banks lure mortgage customers.

When you go to a lender, they like to offer you a carrot. That could be a very low starting interest rate of, say, under 2 per cent. Typically, though, after 12 months, you'll find yourself paying a higher rate. You don't want that. You want to sign up with a low rate that doesn't change unless market forces do — for example, when the Reserve Bank of Australia (RBA) increases rates and the banks pass that increase on. So check for the clauses in the loan contract that aren't so good, or you could end up paying more for that 'special' loan than you'd have paid if you'd gone to another bank in the first place.

The banks may tempt you with an interest-free credit card, frequent flyer points or other rewards. Stay away from these as well. Most people get a credit card these days when they're teenagers. I never had a credit card until I was 36. Typically, if you have a credit card, you've got 50 days interest-free to pay it off. But credit doesn't generally work like that for people who aren't careful with their spending, so you're better off not having a credit card in the first place. That way you avoid any temptation.

So look at that bigger picture right from the start, rather than being diverted by unnecessary extravagance.

A MATTER OF INTEREST

The repayment structure you choose for your loan — whether you opt for an interest-only or a principal-and-interest (P&I) loan — should always be driven by strategy and will depend on both your appetite for risk and your objective.

One of my mortgage brokers, Jerone Balagtas, confirms that since due diligence requires the banks to ensure a borrower pays off their debt in a timely manner in line with their working time frame, banks require any borrower buying a home to live in to take out a P&I loan. This is called an *owner-occupied home loan*, with each loan repayment paying down the balance of the debt.

Another of my trusted mortgage brokers, Fabio De Castro, observes that over the past few years we have seen strong pressure from the regulators for principal-and-interest repayments on owner-occupied properties due to growing concern about high household debt levels in Australia.

WHY AN INTEREST-ONLY LOAN?

When a borrower takes out an interest-only loan, they're not paying down the debt; they're just covering the monthly interest charge.

'We believe', says Fabio, 'that record-low interest rates give a great opportunity to reduce overall non-tax-deductible debt, therefore putting clients in a stronger financial position to continue to build wealth over the long term'.

Jerone points out that, while it is generally in a homeowner's best interests to pay out the loan against their primary residence, other borrowers may take out interest-only loans for cashflow purposes. He says: 'Another reason borrowers may want an interest-only loan is to maximise their future tax strategy through negative gearing. They intentionally keep their loan balance high, as they plan to one day convert their home into an investment property. This is one reason that some banks may consider giving an interest-only loan to a borrower buying their primary residential property.'

Fabio explains: 'Interest-only repayments against the principal place of residence are considered on a case-by-case basis. But even if you get an interest-only loan, it will be a maximum of five years before it automatically reverts to P&I with most lenders. After that point, you must start paying down the principal or request an extension on the interest-only terms with your current lender — which requires a full reassessment of your financial situation. Or you can refinance to another lender.'

The five-year limit for interest-only payments was a result of pressure from the regulators, given their concerns over Australians' high levels of household debt, Fabio observes. 'It is important to note that lenders now assess your ability to repay loans based on the repayments you make once your loan has reverted to P&I, *after the interest-only period*. This strategy ensures that borrowers still have serviceability, as the higher payments have a material impact on household cashflow.'

Jerone explains: 'Banks look at the client's position and will also apply a commonsense approach to a client's objective. As an example, if the borrower has multiple properties and intends to maximise negative gearing, minimise cashflow and can afford to buy more properties and rely on capital growth to build wealth, a bank will understand this borrower to be an experienced property investor. And as long as that borrower's income meets the lending calculation standard, the bank would most likely approve the extension of interest-only repayments.'

THE LENDER'S VIEWPOINT

From a borrowing or refinancing point of view, these days an interest-only loan can leave you with less borrowing capacity in the eyes of lenders. In many cases, it's worth looking outside the major banks, and even at some non-bank lenders. I've often found that the non-bank lenders are far more willing to lend to property investors, who might be running into serviceability issues with the way 'the big four' banks do their calculations.

I built my portfolio with the belief that you should be doing nothing but interest-only loans, but my view has changed a bit in recent years as I've started to consolidate and pick the properties I might keep. As a result, there are some loans that I have moved off interest-only and onto P&I.

I think, okay, I might be keeping those properties for the long term so I'm happy to start paying them down. From an overall portfolio perspective, it depends on the actual property and where it stands in my portfolio. In some cases, banks will insist you pay both principal and interest, or a broker will advise that the right strategy for you is to pay P&I. So always be open to that, and look at the bigger picture.

As an investor, I think it's necessary to pay down your owner-occupied property. You don't want to pay off your investments while you still have an owner-occupied debt. Your money should be going into paying off your principal place of residence because it's a non-tax-deductible loan.

Interest on the investment debt, on the other hand, *is* a tax-deductible expense. If you're paying P&I on that property, then every month you're reducing that loan balance, and as a result your interest cost is also falling, so there'll be less to claim against the investment property. Eventually that property may be positively geared.

Years ago, when I was teaching, I was on PAYG. These days I'm a business owner. When banks look at my income for serviceability, it's complicated, because they're looking at my portfolio of more than 16 properties. They're also looking at my business income and the salaries I pay my staff. Some banks' serviceability calculators vary as well, and that can have side-effects too.

When advising clients, I'm still a big advocate of paying interest-only loans, because they're fully tax-deductible on investment properties. But there are three stages in an investment journey.

LLOYD'S STRATEGY

The three stages of investment:

1. acquisition phase
2. hold phase
3. exit strategy

When we're talking about exit strategy we might start changing the finance around, and that will vary widely from case to case. As I've said, sometimes it's driven by the banks. With bank lending having become tighter in recent years, a few things will be a bit different from when I started building my portfolio in the early 2000s.

FIXED OR VARIABLE INTEREST RATES

This is a bit of a minefield. When you're getting a mortgage, you're often thinking, I need a crystal ball to see which one I should get!

My number one tip is that you can never beat the banks at their own game, so don't go for a fixed rate thinking that's going to solve all your problems. Fixed rates are good because they let you know exactly how much you'll be paying for that mortgage every month over the life of that fixed loan — whether that is 12 months, three years or longer.

However, the fixed rate is usually a bit higher than the variable rate for the same loan, so I advise people to think it over carefully. Look at your cashflow and, if you can afford it, go for a good variable rate. If you can manage that, you're probably going to be better off over the long term.

This is especially true now because, at the time of writing, interest rates are the lowest they have ever been. So definitely shop around. When you have a large portfolio of properties, as I do, I strongly advise against having all your loans with one bank, because the banks then own you, particularly if they start cross-securitising.

I prefer to have no more than two or three loans with the one bank, and to shop around for the next one. As I've mentioned, I don't just check what's being offered by the big four; I also look at some of the non-bank lenders, and spread my portfolio around, thereby mitigating the risk.

OFFSETTING YOUR INTEREST

I also recommend the strategy of buying positive-cashflow properties, which can help you pay off your home more quickly. When the income from the property more than covers the mortgage and other outgoing costs on the investment, any surplus income can be put into the mortgage offset account for your home. It's another way of paying off your home mortgage.

As I've noted, a mortgage offset account is a good thing to have, because it helps you pay down the interest on your loan. So if you owe $500 000 on your home loan and then put $500 000 in your offset account, you're no longer paying any interest on the property. That's the situation I'm in at the moment: I'm not paying any interest on my home in Lilli Pilli right now because I've got a lot of money sitting in the offset account. It's actually fully offset. So if someone asks me what my interest rate is for Lilli Pilli, I can say, 'I'm not paying any interest because I've offset the interest'. The only money I'm paying at the moment is principal, and that means I'll be able to pay off that home loan much faster.

NEGOTIATING A BETTER HOME LOAN DEAL

LLOYD'S STRATEGY

Don't 'set and forget' with your own personal mortgage; talk to your bank some more. Aim to make more regular payments, and review your situation regularly.

If you make a property investment to build wealth, remember to review your financial circumstances often, and do whatever you can to pay off your mortgage as soon as possible. Although you'll often sign up for a 30-year mortgage, no-one actually wants to spend 30 years paying their mortgage off.

While the banks' serviceability requirements can make it difficult to get a loan approved or to refinance — particularly if you have complicated finances or several loans — there are options out there for those seeking a better rate.

If you already have a mortgage, perhaps you're thinking, 'I'll just refinance with a different lender', but the first thing to do is to speak to your own bank, and see if they can give you an interest-rate reduction or a better deal, or if there's anything else they can offer. If you have shown loyalty and always made repayments promptly, then you have a decent shot at negotiating a better rate.

In fact, I advise everyone to check their interest rate regularly and contact their bank to try to negotiate a lower rate, because that's another way to knock years off your mortgage. If you're paying a lower interest rate but keep your repayments higher than they were originally, you can pay more money off your loan.

Another tip for securing a better interest rate on your mortgage is to seek the shortest term possible; that way, you minimise the amount of interest paid. This will increase your monthly repayments, though, so be aware of that and ensure you see the full picture.

🏠💲 A REPAYMENTS FREEZE

If, for whatever reason, you lose your job or have your work hours reduced and you're struggling to pay your mortgage, just contact your bank and ask for a freeze on repayments. You can ask for a three-month or six-month freeze, or even a reduction in payments.

If you're paying off principal and interest, you can change to an interest-only loan. If you're struggling, it's best to be upfront with your lender rather than missing payments, because doing that can leave you with a black mark against your name.

FINANCING MULTIPLE PROPERTIES AND CROSS-COLLATERALISING

Cross-securitisation or *cross-collateralising* properties means you're using security from one property to buy another property. What that means is that the properties are then linked, so if one goes down in value, the bank can force you to sell the *other* property to pay for the one that's fallen in value.

Say you wanted to finance three properties. You wouldn't buy them all with the same bank, because doing so would leave you exposed to that bank. That would actually limit you over the long term. That one lender would end up controlling your investment plans because they control where all your funds are coming from.

If the bank is in control of your wealth-building strategy, that puts you in a bad situation. Quite often the banks will try to sell that as a good thing. If you're trying to create wealth, you want to make sure *you're* controlling the situation, not the other way around. So you need to look at the whole package you're getting from the bank — not just interest rates, but everything they're offering you.

You have to be careful that the banks you're with don't cross-securitise. This means making sure you're using refinancing equity from your properties and your own deposits to buy property, rather than cross-collateralising it with other property you own.

Get a valuation done on the property in which you have equity, then have the bank give you the equity as cash into your bank account. That cash can then be used as the deposit for your next property, and you haven't cross-securitised any properties.

People sometimes cross-securitise their home with an investment property. That's the worst thing you could possibly do, because it could put your home in jeopardy. If something happens with your investment property or if you default on either loan, the bank can just come and take equity from your home or can even claim your home.

All home loan contracts contain a little clause that few people realise is there. It's called the 'all monies' clause, and it basically means exactly that: If you default on your mortgage repayments, the bank can reclaim your properties. It basically means that any security or guarantee will cover all amounts you owe to the bank under any arrangements (including future arrangements), regardless of how they arise.

So be careful which bank you go to, and understand how the finance is set up, because if you've got three or four loans crossed with each other, that can be a massive issue.

CONSTRUCTION LOANS

With complex property investment strategies in which, say, you're buying land then constructing a property on that land, it's particularly important to forward-plan. People's circumstances differ widely. If you don't get the right approval at the start, you could have problems down the road because approvals last for only a certain period of time.

Construction loans are a bit more complicated, because the way they are drawn down is more involved. In most cases, a construction loan involves two contracts. The first covers your purchase of the site, or the land. Then there's a second stage, which involves securing a construction loan via the build contract.

Construction loans are paid in stages. Usually, it's the earthworks, then slab, frames, brickwork et cetera, and you are invoiced by the builder at the completion of each stage. You pass that invoice on to your bank to pay. The interest on your construction loan gradually increases as each stage is paid, until it is fully drawn down on completion of the build. This method of repayment is actually good for your cashflow, as you don't owe the whole loan amount until completion of the build.

Many times I've seen people go to the wrong bank. Some banks restrict lending for construction loans; some have a higher interest rate for construction loans; some will lend a maximum of 70 per cent on construction loans; others will offer only 80 per cent, interest-only construction loans.

This is why it's important to work out in advance whether you can borrow the amount required to complete the land purchase. If you purchase vacant land, with no income on it, you need to put that into your cashflow forecast as well.

A good broker will combine these two contracts as one construction loan. If you're applying for a 'split contract', where you're trying simultaneously to secure one loan to buy the land and another to do construction on it, and you've already got building tenders, you're better off lodging the two applications with the bank in one go, because then they will be assessed and approved as one application.

If you lodge two separate applications, the land will settle but if it takes time to sort out everything with council and the approval for that construction loan expires, you run the risk of having to get the construction loan re-approved. This is sometimes unavoidable and is one of the risks of doing developments.

If, for example, you have the land settled but the build contract doesn't settle until the first progress invoice comes in, that can present a problem. You never know how long council will take to approve construction plans, and this puts you at risk. The finance can expire, or your circumstances can change, or the wider financial industry may even change, and you may not be able to get financed again. You need to factor in these risks and determine whether there are likely to be any changes to your circumstances during the course of your property development.

BACK TO STRATEGY

Ultimately, what kinds of loans you get will come down to what best suits your wealth-building strategy. You need to have a plan for everything you do. It's all about how everything fits in with everything else, how each property fits in with the next property you're going to buy, and how the finances will work to support that.

Planning is how you get there.

CASE STUDY
HOMEOWNERS GENERATE OVER $260 000 INSTANTLY

George and Sarah were both working full-time just to cover the bills and pay off their own home. They had been dreaming of having some extra cash so they could take some time off and go on a few relaxing holidays, as well as buying a few investment properties for their future.

They had the opportunity to use the equity built up in their home to create further income. When they came to me, we discussed a few different strategies and together decided that a duplex project would be the right strategy moving forward to help them achieve their goals. This would give them the quickest and largest return on their investment in the shortest period of time.

By refinancing their family home, they were able to extract enough equity to fund their duplex project. We worked closely with them and their mortgage broker to calculate their true borrowing capacity, so we could identify the most profitable duplex project within their budget.

THE LOCATION

I knew the Newcastle property investment market very well, having gained some excellent results from my own duplex projects and others I had helped my clients develop. This placed me in a strong position to help them.

I educated George and Sarah on the Newcastle market and why, after doing due diligence, I would choose this region for their duplex project. The educational facilities, planned infrastructure, rapidly growing property markets, low tenant vacancy rates and population growth all made this an ideal location to do a duplex project.

I knew this duplex would create high rental yields and instant equity for George and Sarah. These two properties would be positively geared and they could hold on to them for the long term.

NEGOTIATION AND ACQUISITION

Property prices in Newcastle were rapidly increasing, which meant vendors were either holding off on selling their land or asking too much for the blocks.

I had to find a vacant block and ensure a duplex project on it would be approved. After weeks of searching, I found an off-market parcel of land through a real estate agent I'd previously worked with.

We negotiated a reduced price on the land to save the vendor marketing fees. We then tendered out the build project to a few builders who had done quality work for my agency before, and we were able to get a great price with high-quality inclusions.

The total project cost was under $968 722 including the land, build and subdivision. As a result, George and Sarah created $261 278 in equity in less than 12 months. With each unit returning $550 per week, the duplex was providing positive cash flow too. George and Sarah were able to book their holiday and enjoy some quality time together, before they started on their next duplex project with me.

THE NUMBERS

Land:	$295 000
Stamp duty:	$8722
Build costs:	$625 000
Council and subdivision costs:	$40 000
TOTAL COSTS:	**$968 722**
Independent valuations:	
Unit 1:	$610 000
Unit 2:	$620 000
TOTAL:	**$1 230 000**
TOTAL EQUITY AFTER PROJECT COSTS:	**$261 278**

Sarah is a conveyancer and therefore they did not have to pay legal fees as she did the work herself.

CHAPTER 4

BUY YOUR PPOR

Everything you need to know
to buy that home

If you're ready to buy a home to live in, this chapter is for you. It may be your very first home, or you may be upgrading to a larger home. If you're empty nesters, you might be downsizing. We'll explore how to prepare to purchase a home, how to create a comprehensive search brief, and how to find and purchase your principal place of residence (PPOR) for a price that's within your budget.

According to Australian Bureau of Statistics data from August 2019, at any given time almost one in three home purchasers are buying property for the first time.

From a personal perspective, of the properties I've bought for myself and Renee, four have been primary residences, each of which has been an upgrade from the previous one.

From a professional perspective, some people come to me having never owned a property before. I see a lot of couples who bought a little two-bedroom apartment when they first got together, but now they have two kids and are wondering how and where they can afford something bigger.

I never judge. I think people feel they can talk to me and are quite open about their income and circumstances. I take the trust they place in me very seriously. I've got private clients with all levels of income; it makes no difference to me whether they're aiming for a mansion or a modest unit. Whether this is your first home or your dream home, it comes down to figuring out exactly what you want and then working out how to get it on the budget you have.

On the time frame from go to whoa, most finance approvals last for three months before you need to renew them. Ideally, then, you'll aim to get your pre-approval in place and to buy the property within a three-month period. This is why you need to get yourself educated on the markets, to understand what's out there and to be quite clear on what you want before your property search begins.

THE COMPREHENSIVE PROPERTY SEARCH

To help you understand the process of finding the right home for the right price, I'll walk you through our Aus Property Professionals Comprehensive Property Search Service. These are the steps our clients are guided through on the way to finding their new home.

A legitimate budget comes first. Once you have received your financial pre-approval from the broker, we start the search, attending inspections and making recommendations. There's no limit to the number of properties we'll consider on your behalf. We'll work with you until you buy the right property for the right price.

Once we find a suitable property, we try to secure it for a price within your budget. Our due diligence includes market analysis and property assessment. Finally, we initiate negotiations or prepare to bid at auction, if that is how the property is being sold. We don't always get it on the first go, though. We may find the perfect property only to see it exceed our client's budget. For example, we recently found a property that was within the client's budget of $1.6 million, according to our research, so we went to auction to bid for it, but it sold for $1.7 million because the markets were really strong and there was a lot of buyer interest. It can take a few attempts to secure the right property at the right price.

FOUR FINANCING TIPS FOR FIRST HOME BUYERS

We reviewed how to get a mortgage in the previous chapter, but there are a number of other financial elements to consider to make purchasing a home as successful as possible.

1. COMPARE HOME LOANS, AND DON'T BE AFRAID TO REFINANCE YOUR MORTGAGE

A home loan is a long-term debt, so even a small difference in interest adds up over time.

You may consider forgoing a fixed rate and look for a variable rate, as you can't refinance on a fixed rate without paying breakage fees. However, if you're someone who likes the assurance of knowing your exact repayments every month over a fixed period — say, three or five years — then a fixed rate may be for you, especially if you're not planning on selling or refinancing equity out of your home in the immediate future.

Remember, however, that you can never beat the banks at their own game. They will almost certainly foresee things you can't, so it's best not to get locked in for a significant time (such as three or five years).

It's also important to avoid spending more for 'nice-to-have' options. Is it worth paying extra for features you may never use? Make sure the loan suits your lifestyle.

2. THINK LONG TERM ABOUT THE EQUITY

Depending on your long-term goals, you can use the equity you have in your current home for a deposit on another home or investment property. If you're considering this, avoid getting into a situation where collateral for one loan is used as collateral for another loan, as it gives the bank too much control.

You can also use that equity for renovations to add further value to your property. Or, depending on your goals, perhaps pay for private-school tuition for your children or for overseas holidays.

3. MANAGE RISK THROUGH INSURANCE COVER

I always advise people against trying to save on costs by cutting back on insurance, and to always get at least two or three insurance quotes.

- Take out building insurance (or homeowner's insurance), which covers your home for damage caused by fires, storms and floods.

- If you live in a strata title apartment, the entire building will be covered by residential strata insurance.

- Lastly, I recommend taking out contents insurance to cover the repair or replacement of your possessions inside your home.

4. TAKE ADVANTAGE OF GOVERNMENT GRANTS FOR FIRST HOME OWNERS

One of the best ways to get financial assistance with a first-time purchase is by applying for a government grant. The federal government's First Home Owner Grant (FHOG) is a one-off payment to assist first home buyers in purchasing property or building a new residential property for use as their principal place of residence. For information on current Australian government grants visit firsthome.gov.au.

While rising property prices restricted these grants in 2020–21, it's still an option for a large number of Australians. But be aware of the eligibility criteria. You should know, for example, that even if you secure funding via an FHOG, you'll still require a 10 to 20 per cent deposit. Potentially, it can get you into the market faster, but you'll still need to have the finance in place for the type of property you want to buy.

If your partner already owns property, you will not qualify for a FHOG. First home buyers' grant money is also capped at a certain number of people, so the FHOG is not actually open to everyone; it's first in, first served.

Depending on where in Australia you buy, you'll face different requirements and receive different amounts (as well as stamp duty concessions, in some cases). As the legislation changes regularly, you should definitely check your state or territory government sites to keep up with policy changes.

THE GETTING STARTED SESSION

Here's where we discuss your property 'wish list' in detail and finalise the search parameters and budget to create a written brief.

In your wish list you will tell us everything you want in a property, and we'll do our best to match these wishes. In some instances, we'll say, 'Yes, we can get you that'; at other times we'll say, 'We'll try to get that, but we probably won't be able to find such a property within your budget'.

The written brief marks the beginning of the property search. One thing we do *not* do is force our clients to stick to their original brief, as experience has shown us that the search process can often open up possibilities they hadn't previously considered. So you can expect that your brief will evolve as you look at different properties and your knowledge of the markets grow. Some of your initially less important criteria may become 'essential', while others may lose importance.

Have a go at filling out the wish list on the next page. Taking into account everything you might need in a property will give you some real clarity on your requirements and what you're looking for. This wish list is valuable no matter what type of home you're looking to buy. It's all about finding you the right home at the right price.

YOUR WISH LIST

Your TIME FRAME	
When would you like to buy?	
Is there a deadline?	
Your BUDGET (excluding stamp duty)	
What is your maximum borrowing potential?	
What amount are you comfortable spending?	
How much do you think you'll need to spend?	
What is your 'wishful thinking' outcome?	
Your FINANCING	
Do you have pre-approval?	
Will you need a bank valuation?	
Do you have a mortgage broker or bank contact?	
Your DEPOSIT	
A 10 per cent deposit is usually required. How will you be providing this?	
Power of attorney and legal advice	
Do you have a current power of attorney?	
Do you have a solicitor or conveyancer set up?	
What is the most important thing about this move for you?	
Why are you moving?	
Have you seen any properties you like?	
Do you and your partner's criteria differ on any points?	
If this is a family home, please describe your family situation.	
Are you planning on having children?	
Do you have children?	
What ages are they?	
What school(s) do they now attend?	
What school(s) will they attend in the future?	
How will they get to school?	
What are their favourite leisure activities?	
Might strong family ties influence where you buy?	
Do you have pets?	

How long are you planning to live in this home?	
Please list your top six preferred suburbs or areas.	
1.	
2.	
3.	
4.	
5.	
6.	
Are there any other suburbs you have not listed but might consider?	
Are there any suburbs that you have ruled out? If so, for what reasons?	
Your MUST-HAVES	
Number of bedrooms	
Number of bathrooms	
Living areas	
Outdoor space	
Maximum number of levels	
Parking	
Outlook	
What type of property are you looking for?	
Freestanding house	
Semi or duplex	
Apartment	
Townhouse/villa	
External land size	
Level block, or is a sloping block okay?	
Preferred building style and period (e.g. contemporary, Victorian, Federation, Edwardian)	
Number of storeys	
Preferred building material (e.g. brick, rendered, weatherboard)	
External colour, if a consideration	
Condition (Are you prepared to renovate? Would you prefer to do major/little/no work?)	

Title (Torrens [house standard], strata or company)	
Zoning (strictly residential, or mixed residential and commercial)	

Property FEATURES	

Outlook	
What sort of outlook do you want?	
Do you want views?	
If so, views of what?	
From where within the property?	

Aspect	
What aspect would you prefer?	
Where do you want morning and afternoon sun?	
Is there an aspect that does not work for you?	
How important is natural light?	
Where do you most want natural light?	

Security	
Is security important to you?	
Do you want a security alarm system?	
Do you want secure building entrance?	

Parking	
Total parking needs	
Off-street parking	
A lock-up garage	
For how many vehicles?	
For strata, must a car space be on the title?	

Interiors	
Living spaces	
Minimum internal area size	
Minimum ceiling height	
One or more living spaces	
Separate dining room	
Family room	
Study	

Heating and cooling	
Air conditioning (reverse-cycle or ducted)	
Fireplaces	
Gas heating	
Ceiling fans	
Interior finishes	
Floors (boards, carpets, tiles)	
Windows (curtains, blinds, shutters)	
Style (sleek, industrial, traditional)	
Original features (fireplaces, cornices, other)	
Prepared to redecorate?	
Bedrooms	
Sizes (doubles or singles)	
Furniture needs for these rooms	
Alternative use (as a study, TV/media room, library, playroom, other)	
Bathrooms	
Number of bathrooms	
Number of full bathrooms	
Ensuites	
Toilet and basin only	
Bath	
Spa	
Kitchen	
Preferred style	
Open-plan or separate from other rooms	
Preferred benchtop materials (timber, stone, laminate, stainless steel, other)	
Cooktop and oven (induction, gas or electric)	
Butler's pantry	
Other appliances (dishwasher, wall oven, built-in microwave oven, waste disposal)	
Need to install a new kitchen?	

Laundry	
Separate laundry	
Laundry facilities in the kitchen	
Laundry facilities in the bathroom	
External laundry facilities	
Outdoor spaces	
Preferred outdoor spaces (lawn, garden, paved courtyard, deck, balcony)	
Aspect	
Size	
Other features	
Barbecue	
Pool	
Gym	
APARTMENTS	
Building characteristics	
Prefered building size	
Minimum/maximum number of units in the block	
Maximum number of floors	
Preferred level	
Ground-floor apartment	
Maximum quarterly strata levy	
Street and suburb selection criteria	
Type of street you'd like to live on.	
Shops or offices in your street	
Shops or offices in your neighbourhood	
Street and suburb noise	
On or near a main road	
Traffic noise	
Aircraft noise	
Train noise	
Other facilities	
Close to shops	
Schools	

Cafes	
Any other facilities	
Where do you work?	
Do you commute by bus, train, ferry or car?	
Preferred method of public transport?	
How close to public transport do you want to be?	
How far in walking time?	
How close is too close?	
Train, bus, ferry, tram or light rail?	
Are there reasons unique to you that mean you would NOT purchase a specific property? For example, cultural background, mobility issues, allergies or previous experiences in a particular location.	
SUMMARY	
Are you prepared to suspend any of your wish list criteria in order to stay in your preferred suburb, and if so, which items would you be most prepared to give up?	
A bedroom	
A bathroom	
Renovation	
Parking	
Internal living space	
External living space	
Views	
Other	
The absolute ESSENTIALS	
What are the three or four criteria for your property that are most important to you? These are things you won't compromise on. We will eliminate properties from our shortlist if they do not include these essentials.	
The absolute DEAL-BREAKERS	
What are three or four things you *don't* want and that would cause you to walk away from the property? These are also things you won't compromise on.	
Do you have any other comments and/or requirements?	

LLOYD'S STRATEGY

Properties selling via an auction campaign are usually quoted at the bottom of their price guide, so add 20 per cent to get closer to the probable sale price.

PHASE 1: THE PROFESSIONAL PROPERTY SEARCH

Equipped with the brief we put together from your wish list and your approved budget, we begin by conducting a search of available properties that best meet the brief by contacting local real estate agents. As well as 'on-market' properties, they usually inform us of exclusive 'off-market' and 'pre-market' properties. We also look at secondary search areas and find properties that represent compromises (but not deal-breakers) on price, property and position.

From long experience, I have found that almost invariably clients will show us properties they cannot afford and won't get approval for. That's why you get pre-approval up front. If your bank offers you approval for $1.5 million, you can't go and buy a $2 million property. It's also why we take over the property search for you.

The problem is that when a lot of these grand properties go to auction, the agent will tell you, 'The price guide on that is $1.5 million'. So of course you'll think, oh, that's within our price range. But a property is almost always quoted *well below what it is expected to sell for*. That's simply the way it is, and you need to assume the actual sale price will be 20 per cent or more higher than the guide price. The best strategy is to do some serious market research so you know what has been selling in that area recently, and for what price. Go to auctions and speak to agents. Even when I'm helping a client buy their home, I still recommend they get familiar with what the markets are doing.

Everyone starts their property search thinking they can get more than they actually can. But you cannot have champagne on a beer budget. If you have a million dollars to spend but you're looking at properties that have been selling for up to $1.6 million, you're going to keep missing out. My job as a buyer's agent is to help you get what you want for the right price — within your budget.

People often imagine a buyer's agent will magically find them something amazing but cheap, but it doesn't work like that. We can only find what's available and then make sure we get you a great deal on it. That said, one tactic buyer's agents use to discover what properties are available is actually door knocking to see if the resident is thinking of selling their property.

As a buyer's agent, I research, inspect and buy property every day, while the average Australian will buy just one or two properties in their lifetime. One of the key skills of a buyer's agent is to know the markets very well, and to know the true value of properties in a particular suburb. The market knowledge and negotiation skills of a professional will really help you get ahead in what is often a tough market. I never let my clients pay too much for a property.

MUST-HAVES

So when I'm talking about 'buying well', that usually refers to investment properties and considerations, such as 'Don't buy on a busy road or under a flight path', both of which negatively affect the property's long-term growth potential. But when you are buying your principal place of residence, you're not prioritising growth or other investment drivers, as first and foremost this property is a home to live in, which is quite different from a purely financial investment. This is why we ask a lot about your personal preferences — things like whether you're happy to be living on a busy road — so we can build up a picture of your likes and dislikes.

Personally, these days I always consider what sort of growth my home would see, but when I bought my first home in Rockdale that was not the way I looked at it. I wanted a brand-new property that was walking distance from the water and close to transport so I could get into the city easily. And luckily, many of the things I wanted in my first home corresponded with what makes a good investment.

So buying a home means different things to different people, right? It comes down to what you're actually looking for. For families, do you have kids, and if so how old are they? Do you need to get them into a school catchment zone for primary school or a specific local public high school? Or are you planning to send them to private schools, and will they need to be on or close to specific public transport routes to get there?

You might be keen to buy in a school catchment zone now, with the idea that later, when your kids are in high school, you'll upgrade to a different suburb or area and look for something with more space. Such forward planning becomes a part of our strategy.

Say you're looking for a four-bedroom home with a home office, a swimming pool and a double garage on a quiet street. We'll go into detail about inclusions. In the kitchen, do you want 20 mm or 40 mm stone benchtops, 600 mm or 900 mm appliances? What are your lighting preferences, and do you want ducted or split-system air conditioning? Do you want a landscaped backyard, a low-maintenance garden? And so on.

Renovation may be part of the brief. You may say, 'We'd be happy if it's a bit rundown so we can renovate it, especially if it's going to be closer to our budget. Sometimes, though, depending on the location, a need for renovation makes little difference to the price. A well-located property in an area of high demand will often sell at a premium even if it does need work.

 SUBURBS

Once we understand the type of property you want to live in, our next step is to look at the suburbs you prefer and see what you can afford to live in that suburb.

You will have suggested certain suburbs and we'll narrow that down to a shortlist of six, with three 'preferred suburbs' and three others where you might find a home at a slightly lower price point.

We review market activity in those suburbs and show you some comparable sales — that is, sales of properties that are more or less similar to what you are looking for in these areas. We'll tell you what properties have sold for in these suburbs over the past six months. This will give you a realistic sense of what you can expect to pay.

In a very hot market, we need to look especially closely at the sales from the past *two or three months*, as comparable sales from six months ago will be out of date when the markets are moving very fast.

Then we tell you what the market is doing *today*, as it might already have changed slightly. For example, I might say, 'Okay, the market is actually rising, so these properties could already be more expensive than that', or 'The market has dipped a bit lately, so you might get better value for your money in this suburb right now'.

THE SHORTLIST

With the current markets and your budget and timeline in mind, we start looking at properties in the three suburbs that best match your brief, and we draw up a shortlist.

My first move is to call agents to see if they have any upcoming properties that might meet my clients' needs. Agents call me almost every day with properties they've just listed or off-market or pre-market properties that are yet to be listed.

When we find an attractive off-market property we can organise a private inspection, usually during the week, when you may be the first person to see it. You don't need to trawl through open-home inspections on Saturdays. You're not vying with 50 or 100 other potential buyers before auction day.

Sometimes I do recommend that my clients go to an open-home inspection to get a sense of the interest in the property from other potential buyers, especially if the property is listed online. This will help them understand my strategy around the auction and what the place could sell for.

PHASE 2: EVALUATION

Before we can seal that deal, we present you with a full property evaluation. We review all reports and will make you aware of anything that might require further investigation by a solicitor, lender or other expert. To facilitate this, we work closely with your dream team:

1. **We arrange a formal property inspection** through the selling agent and take you to view the property.

2. **We formulate a predictive index for capital growth on the property.** This gives us an objective price benchmark for the property.

3. **We undertake thorough pricing research and provide an individual property report** detailing findings and recent comparable sales.

4. **We devise a purchase strategy using the evaluation information**, to give you the best possible chance of securing the property.

5. **We review the Contract of Sale** and point out any anomalies that might require investigation by your solicitor.

6. **We conduct thorough due diligence on the property, including:**

   - organising a building and pest inspection
   - liaising with council for property searches and obtaining copies of building certificates
   - reporting on any development applications (DAs) on nearby properties
   - organising copies of strata reports, if applicable
   - providing information on aircraft flight paths in the neighbourhood
   - checking for other location-specific issues.

PHASE 3: NEGOTIATION AND PURCHASE

If everything checks out and you are keen to put in an offer for the property, we begin negotiations with the selling agent on your behalf. This may involve:

- negotiating a purchase price on a private treaty sale

- putting in an offer prior to auction

- negotiating counter-offers with the selling agent.

If the property does go to auction:

- we organise the bidding authorisation paperwork

- we undertake the bidder registration process

- I, or one of my team, attend the auction and bid on your behalf.

AUCTION PREPARATION AND BIDDING

We are always prepared weeks in advance. We set a strategy, and all the paperwork must be completed in good time so you can register for the auction.

On auction day, you'll need to bring a driver's licence and have your finances in order, because if we are the successful bidders you will need to pay the deposit (5 or 10 per cent) by cheque or be able to transfer the funds directly into the selling agent's trust account then and there.

Usually you will accompany us to the auction. If you are interstate or overseas, you will likely be on the phone with me throughout the auction.

My auction tactics have changed a bit since I wrote my previous book, *Positively Geared*. I used to be pretty set in the way I did auctions, but nowadays I play it more by ear. Every auction is different. So sometimes I'll be the first to bid, sometimes not. Sometimes I'll just watch what others are doing and get a feel for things. It partly depends on the bidding increments and on how many people are present. If there are not too many people, I still usually try to control things.

No matter what, I arrive in a suit while everyone else is wearing casual clothes, and I *always* have my poker face on. Some people inadvertently give the game away. I've been at auctions where people are talking among themselves and they're smiling, and I can tell they're at the end of their budget. No-one can tell what my bidding budget is. If I had just $1000 left in reserve, I'd still bid that, and no-one would have a clue I was down to my last dollar.

I'll give you an example from my own experience: My client was on the phone from Brisbane while I was bidding on their behalf at an auction in Sydney. Before the end I told them with total confidence, 'Yeah, we've got this one'. I could see the other bidders were at the end of their budget, which was confirmed when their mother leaned in and said, 'Oh, bid a bit more. I'll lend you another $10 000'. I shouldn't have known that about them, but they let it slip, which was a rookie mistake. It was just inexperience. I told my client, 'We can bid another $5000 and we'll have it, because they're finished'.

EMOTIONAL PURCHASES

It pays to have a professional bid for you, especially when the purchase is an emotional one, such as when you're buying a home for yourself or your kids.

I never get emotional; I just play my game. I know we can't go above the limit, and some things you can't control. For example, I went to an auction in Newcastle recently and the property sold for $300 000 above the price guide to a guy who was buying it for his 18-year-old daughter. She was starting university and the house was within walking distance of the campus, so he just kept bidding until he outbid everyone else.

Because I was bidding for a client, there was no way I was going to pay too much for the property, but this guy just kept bidding and bidding. He obviously had money, and he evidently felt committed. Suddenly Newcastle was setting new records for house prices! At times like that there's nothing you can do about it. Emotion-based bidding drives up the price of property, as it did at that auction.

I don't need to talk to you between every incremental bid during an auction, because we discussed the strategy beforehand. We know the budget, so I say nothing except to make the bids. It's only when we get to the very end of their budget that I might say (quietly), 'Can we just go another thousand, or another five thousand? Because if we do, I think we'll get it'. Before that, no conversation — it's all business.

When clients get emotional at auctions, I tell them to put their poker face on. Most of the time they tell me afterwards that they were pretty nervous. They didn't know what was happening because *they* couldn't read me either.

Once the gavel falls at an auction, the highest bidder owns the property. There's no cooling-off period. Everyone claps, and the winning bidders go inside to sign the contract and pay the deposit — and that home is theirs.

Some find the bidding game very stressful, but to me it's fun. I love auctions. They're actually a very transparent way of selling property.

PRE-SETTLEMENT INSPECTION

When we buy a property, whether it is by auction or private treaty, we organise access to the property with the selling agent again, and perform a thorough inspection just before the settlement date to ensure that all contract inclusions are present and that the property is in the same condition as when it was offered for sale.

SETTLEMENT DAY

On settlement day, at an agreed time, your solicitor or conveyancer facilitates the transaction, with your lender and the seller's representatives exchanging documents. They will organise for the balance of the purchase price to be paid to the seller. Your lender will register a mortgage against the title of the new property, providing the funds for you to purchase the property.

The solicitor or conveyancer checks that:

- any existing mortgage on the title to the vendor is discharged

- any rights over the property of a third party or person (called a caveat) are removed

- all clauses in the sales contract are fulfilled

- the transfer of land and mortgage is registered with the Titles Office in your state or territory.

Then you receive the keys.

SEVEN TIPS FOR SECURING YOUR HOME PURCHASE

To buy successfully like a buyer's agent, you need to take the initiative every step of the way, and to be prepared and flexible.

1. BE PROACTIVE WITH FINANCE

Ensure you have your pre-approval before commencing your property search, so you don't miss out on properties while submitting your paperwork and waiting for banks or brokers to get back to you.

If your finance is ready to go, you'll have the option of making an unconditional offer (with no extra clauses or special conditions added). You'll also be aware of any other conditions the seller has included in the contract, so where possible you can accommodate these for a greater chance at success.

2. BE KNOWN TO LOCAL AGENTS

If you're ready to go, reach out and get in touch with local agents. Let them know your buying criteria and budget, ask to be contacted with off-market opportunities and when new properties are listed. Ask to be added to their mailing list, so you're one of the first to know about new listings and to inspect a suitable property when it becomes available.

3. BRING A CHECKLIST TO VIEWINGS

Do your research on the asking price of the property, as well as recent sales of comparable properties, so you can anticipate what the property will sell for. Have a clear list of absolute deal-breakers and absolute must-haves, so you can decide if the property is suitable immediately upon viewing.

4. SUBMIT AN OFFER IN WRITING

Be decisive and submit a clear offer in writing as soon as practicable after viewing the property. This will demonstrate that you are serious and leave no room for the property to be snapped up while you think about it for a few days.

5. GET YOUR OFFER SEEN

Your offer should be reasonable, so consider the current market conditions. If you offer a low-ball price, unless the seller is prepared to negotiate it's unlikely you'll come to an agreement to proceed. Game Over.

If you have offered close to but below the asking price the seller is likely to ask for an increase. However, if your research shows that the property is worth only what you have offered, then stand your ground.

6. NO COOLING OFF

An offer subject to cooling off will be less attractive to the seller than an unconditional offer, just as an offer with fewer or no conditions will be more attractive than one subject to multiple conditions. Removing a cooling-off period shows the seller you are serious.

7. GOOD TERMS

If your terms are aligned with the seller's requirements and are uncomplicated, with few restrictions, your offer may appear more attractive, even if it is lower than the asking price.

Being able to offer flexible terms such as unconditionality, or terms accommodating a longer or shorter settlement period if the seller requests it, or being agreeable to deposit release if this is requested, will work in your favour.

What doesn't work? Leaving the seller waiting for follow-up calls. If you have viewed a property and are serious about purchasing it, you will need to make contact right away.

CASE STUDY
PRE-MARKET OPPORTUNITY SECURED IN A HOT MARKET

Glen and Brooke, a busy couple with a young family, were looking to buy a home in Sydney's southern suburbs. They had spent months scouring the internet for potential properties within their $1.6 million budget, and much of their spare time at open homes. They wanted their Saturdays back! Frustrated, they reached out to my team.

GETTING STARTED SESSION

Glen and Brooke had been living in Sydney's southern suburbs for a number of years but, with a second child on the way, they had outgrown their current home. They needed a minimum of three bedrooms, two bathrooms and one car space or on-street parking.

THE CHALLENGES

Glen and Brooke's children were enrolled in a local school, so it was vital for the family to stay in the area. They also needed to be close to public transport and shops, but didn't want to live on a main road.

The properties they had been looking at were advertised for below their maximum budget of $1.6 million, with price guides of $1.3 to $1.5 million. But with huge buyer demand, prices for comparable properties in the area were being pushed well above what these properties had been advertised for. In a fast-moving seller's market, price guides often don't keep up with market demand.

GLEN AND BROOKE'S BRIEF (FROM THEIR WISH LIST):

Price range: $1.6 million

Deadline: Six months

Primary suburbs: Rodd Point, Five Dock, Russell Lea, Wareemba, Abbotsford

Glen and Brooke's parents lived in the shire, and they wanted to be close to them. These suburbs were less congested than most in the area, with wider streets and on-street parking for the family's two cars.

Secondary suburbs: Drummoyne (west side of Victoria Road), Concord, Haberfield and parts of Leichhardt and Lilyfield that are close to the Bay Run and away from aircraft noise.

What's important (essential criteria):

1. Good location

2. Good lifestyle and walkability

3. Space to upsize the property

(continued)

4. Outdoor backyard area

5. Street parking

Deal-breakers:

1. Major main or congested roads

2. Absence of street parking

3. No room to renovate or upsize

4. Not feeling safe in the area—for instance, in an industrial area

Noise preference: No traffic noise (some aircraft noise okay)

Building type: Freestanding or semi-detached brick home in any style

Happy to renovate? Yes

Land size: 280 square metres or more

Aspect: North-facing backyard

Bedrooms: Three

Bathrooms: Two

Car spaces: One

Mobility: No steep stairs at entrance preferred (for the grandparents)

Places of work: Brooke: CBD and home; Glen: Parramatta HQ and Homebush site office

Travel to work: Brooke: ferry or bus; Glen: car

Children: A two-year-old and a new baby due in December

Kids' schools/childcare: Childcare is in Five Dock but can move her to another if needed. Primary school is in Five Dock.

THE PROPERTIES THAT CAME CLOSEST TO MEETING GLEN AND BROOKE'S BRIEF

We found a number of suitable properties that were mostly in line with the couple's brief, including the following:

RODD POINT

Accommodation: 3 bed / 1 bath / 1 car

Land size: 360 square metres

Date sold: 5 June

Price: $1 415 000

Notes: Freestanding, renovated, scope to add value, in a preferred location

Recommend? Yes

Client comments: Like the location, land size, scope to add value, potential to add parking.

RUSSELL LEA

Accommodation: 3 bed / 1 bath / 2 car

Land size: 246 square metres

Date sold: 16 April

Price: $1 460 000

Notes: Compromised floorplan, small bedrooms, poor indoor/outdoor flow, thoroughfare position, south aspect

Recommend? No

FIVE DOCK

Accommodation: 3 bed / 1 bath / 0 car (street parking)

Land size: 348 square metres

Date sold: 4 May

Price: $1 470 000

Notes: Preferred location, requires cosmetic renovation, then later a more extensive renovation, no off-street parking

Recommend? Yes—pending inspection

Client comments: We would renovate cosmetically just to move in for five years, so would buy this one and try to find parking.

As well as properties that met the brief, we showed Glen and Brooke 20 other properties that were a fairly close match but meant compromising on price, position or property style. One of these was in Rodd Point.

(continued)

RODD POINT

Accommodation: 4 bed / 2 bath / 2 car

Land size: 382.9 square metres

Date sold: 24 March

Price: $1780000

Notes: Preferred location, good curb appeal, functional floorplan, south aspect, no undercover parking

Recommend: Yes

Client comments: Love space and location. Exceeds required bedrooms, which is great.

Glen and Brooke fell in love with this property, which had a price guide of $1.4 million. It was an older build but semi-renovated and well presented. As Brooke and Glen's budget was $200000 above the price guide, this seemed an achievable property.

But even that older property sold for $1.78 million—a whopping $380000 more than the price guide! This was simply because of the markets we were working with.

THE RESULT

One thing Glen and Brooke had never thought possible was buying themselves a brand-new home, so when our team presented them with a stunning new build in the St George area of Sydney, with four bedrooms, not two but three bathrooms, and a remote-controlled lock-up garage, they tried not to get their hopes up.

Through one of our many agent contacts, we were able to get pre-market access to the property. And with Glen and Brooke financially prepped and ready to pounce, they made an offer that day. We negotiated the sale for $1.6 million, the day before the property was due to go live to the public.

Afterwards, Glen and Brooke told us: 'We are dead sure that without the work of the APP team we would have had many more weeks, perhaps months, of frustration ahead of us, as well as the distinct possibility of ending up in a worse property or having to pay significantly more—likely both!'

THE NUMBERS

Property purchase price:	$1 600 000
Stamp duty:	$72 862.40
Legal fees:	$1800
Building and pest inspection:	$660
TOTAL PURCHASE COSTS:	**$1 675 322.40**
Independent valuation results:	
After just 18 months, the property was revalued at	$2 550 000
TOTAL IMPROVED EQUITY AFTER COSTS:	**$874 677.60**

CHAPTER 5

BUY YOUR DREAM HOME

*Get ready to take the investment journey
of a lifetime*

 I talk a lot about the dream home as a 'big life goal', because for so many people, myself included, it is indeed a major aspiration. And I love to teach people how to get there. In this chapter, I'll share why I believe you should be prepared to make some compromises today in order to start investing in property earlier, so you can get to that dream home down the track sooner. I know you can do it because that's how I reached my own dream home goal.

One thing I'm sure of: if I hadn't been successful in property investing, I wouldn't have been able to use those investments to help me get my waterfront dream home in Sydney's Lilli Pilli.

Many people struggle with that. They come to me and say, 'I just want the great Australian dream — a freestanding house on a quarter-acre block — but I only earn this much so can't afford that. How do I get from here to there?'

So many people want that dream home *now*, straight away. After all, their parents could do that back in the 1980s, when you could buy a big house with a backyard for $70 000. My parents bought their farm in Orange for $20 000 in the 1970s. But that sort of opportunity just doesn't crop up these days.

Skyrocketing house prices and inflation have changed things. House prices really took off in Australia in the mid 1990s. Prior to that, in 1990, a house might cost about four times someone's annual income, and typically you could pay off your home in 10 to 15 years. In Sydney things were already getting hard: in 1990 the median house price was $192 348, which was eight times the average wage of $24 000.

Today, if you're making the average Australian wage of $78 000 a year and you decide to buy a $1.2 million house, that's *15 times* your salary. You'll pay around $5000 a month (or $60 000 a year) in mortgage repayments, and it will still take 30 years (at a 5 per cent interest rate) to pay it off. In fact, there's no way a bank will grant you a loan of that size on your salary, because after you've shelled out $60 000 in mortgage repayments and about $15 000 in tax, you would have just $3000 of your annual salary left to live on.

This example illustrates the difference in scale between incomes and house prices in the 2020s, compared with those in the seventies, eighties and early nineties, when the gap between the two was less extreme.

It's generally considered that paying 30 per cent or more of your income on your mortgage every month is too much. When you add in your household expenses — looking after kids, buying food, paying the bills and so on — you'll end up on the breadline. That's called 'mortgage stress'.

LLOYD'S STRATEGY

Keep your mortgage repayments to no more than 20 per cent of your income.

You need to stay in your comfort zone, where you pay 15 to 20 per cent (or less) of your income on your mortgage. For example, I pay only about 10 per cent of my monthly income to cover my repayments.

So if you are an average income earner and your big goal is to buy your dream home, you're going to have to work up to it, and the only way to do so is by increasing your income, whether through a better paying job or through savvy investments — or, as in my case, both.

WHERE TO START

LLOYD'S STRATEGY

Understand what you can get for your money and go from there.

Unless you're fortunate enough to be able to buy a house outright, you will need a mortgage, and there's a limit to how much the bank will lend you. Even on a couple-combined income of $150 000 a year, you're unlikely to be able to afford your dream home right away — otherwise everyone would be doing it!

You may have a budget of $800 00 for a first home and want to buy in Sydney. Sadly, you can't buy a house for that in Sydney anymore, so you end up buying an apartment.

Neither can you expect to buy a unit and then, a few years later, buy a house, before jumping to your dream house. I had four different homes, culminating with the dream home that Renee and I have now.

My first property, that tiny one-bedroom apartment in Rockdale, was all I could afford back then. It was a start. My second property, in Ingleburn, was larger but a long way out. In the car it took two and a half hours to get to the school where I worked at in the eastern suburbs. But, again, that's what I could afford at the time, knowing it was a stepping-stone to my next, bigger and better place. Of course, I was single then. A young family would find it hard to be so flexible, and that's where strategies like rentvesting or making a sea change, come in, which I'll talk about in this chapter.

DON'T BLOW YOUR DEPOSIT

I think there's a lot of FOMO among potential investors when the markets start booming. That's something I talk about a lot: whenever the market heats up, people worry they're going to miss out on a great opportunity.

As soon as prospective investors have saved their deposit, they often feel they have to rush in and buy. You may be sitting on $160 000 in savings, but you don't need to spend it all on one property, especially if you're simply putting that money down on something you can afford. It's about *strategy*. You could diversify by spending that amount on a couple of cheaper properties. You might also be able to take out another loan to buy another property. So you could do a 90 per cent deposit on two properties and leverage your lending to different locations.

Often people are confused about what the markets are doing. They ask me, 'Is now the right time to buy?' They've got the mortgage green light but don't want to start looking because they're confused about what location to buy in and scared they won't find the right property within their budget. Some worry about paying too much or aren't sure what to buy.

I don't tell people they can't have their own home. 'It's great to have your own home', I say, 'but if it's going to stop you from reaching your goals, you have to factor that in.' Then I bring them back to their goals', and we focus on those.

When potential new clients come to me, the first thing they ask is, 'Can we discuss what services you offer?' As you now know, the first thing I always ask them is, 'What are you hoping to achieve over the next five, 10 or 15 years?'

Most buyer's agents will say, 'These are our services. We can help you buy a property. Where do you want us to look? We'll go out and find it'. And most of the good ones should be able to find you a property, right? But I do a lot more than that, because my focus is far beyond purchasing that property. I want to understand a client's long-term goals and then help them build a portfolio that will ensure they achieve those goals.

For example, if your long-term goal is financial security when you retire, it makes more sense to invest in a number of properties than to spend all your money on a great home now, because rather than providing financial security, that home is a liability, and you'll end up just paying off the mortgage. If anything happens to your job or income, you won't be able to afford the repayments anyway.

If you have a portfolio of investment properties with positive cashflow and something happens to your job, you've still got your properties, which basically look after themselves while providing you with a passive income.

Still, some people just want to buy a home to live in, and I'll help them with that. What we'll look at will depend on their circumstances, what they can afford and what they want. If their goal is to buy a unit close to the city, we'll focus on that. We'll discuss what the mortgage will be, and how much the strata will add to that cost, then we'll compare that strategy with alternatives, such as buying a house a little bit further out. We'll weigh up the pros and cons of that option, because further from the city centre, if they're careful, they could probably get a bit more for their money.

Most of the time they know where they want to live. They can work that out for themselves. I'm not a life coach; I can't really advise people on it. All I'm doing is helping them clarify what they want and can afford, then sourcing suitable properties.

After I've laid out their options, a lot of clients end up deciding to buy an investment property — usually one that's positively geared and has some value-add opportunity (subdivision, development or renovation potential). They are willing to forgo buying a home today so they can build up their equity and can afford to buy a better home tomorrow.

I still own the Armidale duplex that gave me that big 'aha moment' when I first realised the magic of equity creation. It has always been cashflow-positive, and that rental money is part of my income, which now pays the mortgage on my dream home.

USING INVESTING TO GROW YOUR NEST EGG

To secure your dream home in the 2020s, you will probably need to build an investment portfolio and set an exit strategy, which will mean selling some of your properties to pay down the debt on others. Ultimately it will be your exit strategy that helps you secure your dream home.

As I've explained, a home is not necessarily a good first investment, especially if you find you're then working to pay the mortgage and can't afford to do anything else (*mortgage stress*). But if you invest first, and your tenants are covering most or all of your mortgage repayments, you can build up a portfolio that will help you afford a better home later.

In a nutshell, if you have a steady rental income stream from your investment property, the banks will usually let you borrow more money. As discussed in chapter 3, this improves your serviceability — your ability to pay a mortgage. If you buy a home first it's a liability, and because you're paying the mortgage yourself, it'll be tougher (depending on your income) to borrow more. That's how so many people get stuck at one property and can't get any further.

You can also find yourself trapped if you're selling and buying in the same inflated market: you might get more for the property than you paid for it, but you're also paying more for the *next* property.

LLOYD'S STRATEGY
Remember the
property trifecta

EQUITY   CASHFLOW   GROWTH

For clients with lower incomes, we recommend a better strategy: build a portfolio of properties to *create cashflow and equity*.

We always look for the property trifecta of growth, equity and cashflow. It's important to find properties to which we can add immediate value, but they should also generate good cashflow. For some of the properties there will be an exit strategy to sell down, which will then create the profit needed to pay the deposit on the bigger, better home our clients really want.

The next few chapters speak specifically to 'beginner investors' and will shed light on the best strategies to start with, while building up the deposit you'll need to get to your dream home.

REGIONAL AREAS ARE KEEPING THE 'GREAT AUSTRALIAN DREAM' ALIVE

In Sydney, a million dollars won't get you very far in property. This is why we are hearing so much about people needing to downsize their ambitions — because they generally can't afford properties in Australia's bigger cities.

If you're prepared to get out of the 'big smoke' and go to the right regional area, you can still achieve that great Australian dream of a spacious family home with a big backyard. There are lots of opportunities in regional areas. Those markets are really opening up due to their relative affordability, and they're great for families.

We saw many more people moving out of Sydney and Melbourne and other capital cities in 2020 and 2021. I believe that trend will continue and even grow over the next few decades.

For the most part, people who move to regional areas aren't expecting to pick up a mansion out in the country. It's about finding an area they like and buying a nice home there. For some it's also about a 'tree change'.

WHY AND WHERE?

Wondering if you're up for a tree change? That still comes down to where you see yourself in five, 10 or 20 years' time, and why you want to move. Which comes back to strategy, advice and expectations. It's important to have those conversations so your *why* can inform your *where*. Think about your goals, along with those for your kids. Will moving help or hinder your achievement of those goals?

Your work situation will usually affect where you move to. Can you work remotely and commute a couple of days a week? Can you start your own business from home? Can you find work where you plan to move?

Moving to a new town or rural location can be isolating, especially if you have young children. If you currently have family and friends nearby, will the big change remove your support network? One of the reasons we chose to move to Lilli Pilli was to be near Renee's parents, who are now very involved grandparents.

Perhaps you have elderly or not-so-well parents to look after. That's another big consideration. If you're moving away from your hometown, does that take your parents out of the equation? Or are you moving so you can be *closer* to family or friends?

It also helps to clarify what you're looking to achieve with a regional property. With home purchases, growth potential doesn't matter so much. For example, if you're living in Marrickville in Sydney, where for $800 000 you'd be lucky to get yourself a one-bedroom apartment, you might consider moving to Muswellbrook in NSW, where you can buy a four-bedroom house on a nice big block for around $450 000. If it's a home purchase, I'd say go for it if you like the area and want to live there. But if you're looking at it as an investment, I'd advise against it, because Muswellbrook relies heavily on mining and is therefore a 'boom-bust' market.

If you want to live in the property in the short term then rent it out down the track, look at areas with good growth potential. I've had clients move to high-growth locations they like — Byron Bay, Lennox Head or the

Sunshine Coast, for example — and build a duplex there so they can keep one unit to live in and rent out or sell the other.

People are buying in those well-loved coastal areas because Sydney has become too expensive, but all this relocation has pushed up property values in those areas too. Prices in some parts of Byron Bay are now higher than in many parts of Sydney.

THE 'RENTVESTING' STRATEGY

If you're a big-city person and can't bear the thought of moving away from the hustle and bustle, *rentvesting* may be a better option. Rentvesting means renting a property where you want to live while investing in an area you can afford. So rather than purchasing in your favourite suburb, rent there while you build up some wealth on the side. Rent used to be seen as 'dead money', but these days more and more people are adopting this strategy.

If you're leasing out your investment property, then you're not paying anything on your mortgage for that property because your tenant is covering it (provided it's positively geared). You can be comfortable knowing that your rent is less than a home-loan repayment, and you still get to live where you want to.

This provides much more 'disposable income', and you can utilise your serviceability to invest in growing markets elsewhere.

CASE STUDY
MARY HAD $1 MILLION TO INVEST IN PROPERTY IN SYDNEY

A recent client, Mary, in her late forties, had a $1 million approval from the bank and was desperate to buy her own home in the Sydney market. I convinced her to invest in several properties that would create an income stream and later offer security for her retirement.

(continued)

She wasn't looking for her dream home; she just wanted to get out of where she was living and buy her own home.

Before she came to me, Mary had been debating whether to buy a home or an investment property. If I'd agreed to help Mary buy her own home, she would either be living somewhere affordable where she didn't really want to be, or have paid $1 million for a unit in Carlingford, losing more than 30 per cent of her income on repayments.

I talked her out of that. We set up an investment strategy that allowed her to use her $1 million to buy two investment properties, both of which were cashflow positive, which put her in a much better financial position. Beyond her deposit, it wasn't going to cost her anything!

Mary ended up rentvesting in Carlingford, close to where her family lives. In Carlingford at the time, it would have cost her around $1.5 million to buy a house, so she couldn't have afforded to buy a home there, but she *could* afford to rent there.

The other reason I advised Mary against investing in Sydney is because it has the lowest rental yields in the country. She invested in a property in Newcastle and another in Brisbane; both offered good growth and, more importantly, higher rental yields.

So although she had wanted to buy in the peaking Sydney market, Mary ended up investing in growing markets with plenty of scope for her properties to increase in value. She wasn't financially 'maxed out' and stuck with paying off one expensive property, and she was much better off in terms of cashflow, having invested in regions with better rental yields. She had $800 000 in mortgages, but her tenants' rent covered her repayments.

Mary has decided to continue to rentvest in the area she loves, all the while building up a nest egg for the future. Here are the numbers on the two investment properties she purchased.

(continued)

THE NUMBERS

Property #1 location: Newcastle

Property purchase price:	$550 000
Stamp duty:	$19 957
Legals:	$1550
Building and pest inspection:	$660
TOTAL PURCHASE COSTS:	**$572 167**
Rent:	$600 per week
Gross yield:	5.67 %
Annual growth:	17 %

Property #2 location: Brisbane

Property purchase price:	$450 000
Stamp duty:	$15 457
Legal fees:	$1550
Building and pest inspection:	$660
TOTAL PURCHASE COSTS:	**$467 667**
Rent:	$540 per week
Gross yield:	6.24 %
Annual growth:	13 %

UPSIZING TO YOUR DREAM HOME

If you're making a bit more money and have built up some good equity in your investments or family home, you can afford a better property in a suburb where you want to live.

Renee and I bought our Lewisham property soon after we met, and some people thought we were putting the cart before the horse, but I was confident because I knew she was the one! Besides, our agreement was that we would both contribute to paying down the mortgage, but I would pay the deposit and she would choose and pay for all the nice furniture.

It was the last property we lived in before we bought our dream home in Lilli Pilli. Back then I was buying lots of investment properties, but she did all the research on our homes. Happy wife, happy life. So it was Renee who discovered the house.

We had looked at a few homes. This one was on a horrible road — it was the sort of place I'd never normally buy. But it was really nice inside. It was 100 years old but completely renovated and it looked brand-new, so that worked for me as I prefer to live in new properties.

This house stood on a block size of 282 square metres — more than double the size of most houses in the area, with a relatively large backyard. When we were sitting outside in the backyard, we couldn't even hear the traffic on the busy road. In the bedrooms, traffic noise was a bit of a pain, but other than that it didn't really bother me, other than making it a bit more challenging for resale.

We bought it and moved in. We were engaged three months later and married 12 months after that. Renee was still working in auditing in the city, and we loved to go to bars and restaurants there after work.

OUR DREAM HOME: LILLI PILLI

While we were living in Lewisham we had considered buying our dream home. We began by looking at whether we should buy some land and build. But there would have been quite a time frame around that: we'd have had to buy a property, knock down a house, get a development application, have an architect design the home and send the plan to the local council for approval. And then start the build.

Another option we considered was leaving Sydney for a year. We would do a road trip up north, work remotely and rent a house on the beach in Newcastle.

We also started looking at various locations we liked in Sydney — the eastern suburbs and Hunters Hill — but Renee really wanted to moved back to the Sutherland Shire, where she grew up. We ended up buying in Lilli Pilli because it's a really lovely location, but more than anything it was the house itself we fell in love with.

THE PROPERTY SEARCH

Once we'd decided on our preferred location, we started by inspecting a few properties that came up in the Shire. It was very interesting because the region includes semi-regional suburbs as well as urban areas and places by the water.

We *really* wanted a home on the waterfront. We also wanted a bigger house with more bedrooms because we wanted to start a family. Lewisham didn't have a garage, and it had parking for only one car in the driveway — the road outside was too busy to park on — so a home with a double garage was now a must for us.

We looked at a lot of expensive waterfront properties in several suburbs, including Burraneer, Lilli Pilli, Port Hacking and Sylvania, and didn't really like any of the houses we saw. Then Renee came across this house.

We had looked at four or five other properties already that day, and I was a bit tired of inspections, but Renee had seen the property online and was excited, so we went to the inspection.

I thought grumpily, oh, more of the same thing. Do we really need a property this big? And that was kind of that. But afterwards I got to thinking about the place, and I realised it was actually really nice. So I went back.

I ended up doing quite a few more inspections and absolutely fell in love with it. It's unique. We're on the waterfront, and it has huge windows with elevated water views. And the garage is above the house. I've never found any other house with that kind of design. It's a six-bedroom property so there's plenty of room to bring up kids — even a bit of overkill. But we've got a big kids' playroom, which could be used as a music room in the future, Renee and I are both still in orchestras, and there's a games room downstairs as well.

I remember speaking to my mortgage broker Fabio to get our finance started and informing him that this was the start of an auction campaign, with the auction coming up in a month's time. Renee and I were scheduled to be in Bali that weekend, so I was considering getting someone else to bid for me, but I was worried we might miss out. So we postponed our Bali trip by a week, and I went to the auction myself.

I kept my poker face on — but only just! You can read about that in *Positively Geared*.

With a three-month settlement period, we had plenty of time to sell our old house before moving in. Renee's parents didn't say much at first, but I think they were very excited. I know Renee's dad loves it, because he's always standing at the window looking out at the water views.

When deciding on Lilli Pilli, being close to Renee's parents was definitely in the back of our minds. This was before we had kids, but now with the two little ones we realise how important it is to be close to their grandparents. Lewisham was a long way from Renee's parents, but we see them all the time now, which is good. It's also a lot more accessible than Lewisham for my brother and my mum, who come down to Sydney from Orange through the Blue Mountains.

I was planning on keeping Lewisham when we were moving to Lilli Pilli, but as it was an older house, the upkeep was high. So I decided to sell and use the profits to help buy Lilli Pilli.

We'd assumed you had to live near the city to have good cafes and restaurants nearby, but since moving to the Shire, Renee and I have discovered really nice restaurants in Cronulla, so we still have that lifestyle available to us. Lewisham was quite good for parties, but at Lilli Pilli the house itself is a lifestyle. You don't really need to leave for anything!

So it took a good deal of hard work and dreaming, strategies and compromises to get here, but yes, we have our dream home now.

Everyone's dream home is different. Living by the beach might be a dream for some people, but others might dream of a home near a nice park, or an inner-city apartment, or maybe a beautiful farm. Some people don't mind living on a busy road or close to a railway line. Whatever *your* dream home is, that's what you should be aiming for.

CASE STUDY
ENGAGEMENT TO EXCHANGE IN FOUR DAYS!

Jerry and Wendy are a busy professional couple with a young family who have outgrown their current family home. They had been searching for their new 'dream home' without much success. They had already missed out on several properties they loved. When another ideal family home was about to go to auction, they decided to give themselves an advantage by hiring a professional property negotiator, giving themselves the best possible chance of securing the property before the auction. So they reached out to Aus Property Professionals.

We provided them with an in-depth property assessment and a personalised strategy for the purchase of that property. This service took away the worry of potentially making a bad decision and gave them the confidence to move forward with the purchase process.

THE RESULT

Jerry and Wendy had their eye on a four-bedroom, three-bathroom, three-car home in Sydney's south. The property guide was for offers over $1.9 million. At the time the property was going to auction, the market was on fire because of the pandemic property boom, and property prices were soaring, so it was very likely that the property price would end up well over the price guide.

As I've said, at auctions, emotions tend to run high. Family-home buyers can become very attached to a property and develop that 'got to have it' mindset. As a consequence, many of them will go well over their budget to secure the property they've fallen for.

Jerry and Wendy had a budget of $2 million. It was apparent that an auction would not be the ideal situation for acquiring the property, as it would likely sell for higher than their budget would allow. The Aus Property Professionals team conducted all due diligence to enable us to evaluate and formulate a pre-auction strategy. We went in

(continued)

with all boxes ticked and negotiated with the selling agent to secure Jerry and Wendy their dream home—for $1.875 million—on the day before the property was to go to auction.

The entire process, from engaging our services to the exchange of contracts, took just four days!

CHAPTER 6
BECOME AN INVESTOR

For new investors, the time to buy is right now

Almost one in two Aussies name property as their first choice when it comes to investing, but many feel overwhelmed by the number of steps required to purchase a property. In this chapter, we will discuss the disincentives to investing, look at some of the most common mistakes made by first-time investors, and present a simple, step-by-step guide to becoming a successful investor.

Taking the plunge into property investment can be a daunting proposition for those who haven't done it before. The myriad factors that must be taken into account can quickly cause information overload. There are a few things you need to understand about the major disincentives to property investment so you're not held back.

RISK AVERSION

People feel daunted by the perceived risks. Property may be the ultimate risk–reward investment, but the success stories of those who found a pathway to financial freedom far outweigh the failures. And while we do sometimes make poor investment choices and lose money, especially when we're starting out, many Australians who've jumped into the property market over the past 20 to 30 years have done fine, without a huge amount of downside or risk.

Risk-averse people often focus on what can go wrong rather than what can go right. We hear of people being warned off property investment by someone with an overly risk-averse opinion but without a full grasp of the facts.

Avoiding failure is all about fully understanding the investment you're making and performing due diligence so that any decision you make is based on solid research (chapter 10 focuses on due diligence).

What I hear all too often is how many people regret *not* having made a property purchase years earlier, before the market took off. 'If only I had moved then ...!' If all those people had done their research and understood the risks, they would be well on their way to financial independence by now.

ANALYSIS PARALYSIS

It's not just about crunching the numbers; it's also about understanding *where* to invest. There are lots of places you could invest and a heap of information out there to help you decide.

You can extract all sorts of advice from property experts, attend property seminars, read the newspapers, even speak with people you know who have property. It seems like everyone's got something to say on this subject, but understand that many of them are pushing their own agenda, and that may confuse you, scare you off or trigger 'analysis paralysis'.

Keep in mind that 'free' advice is not necessarily good advice and comes with its own costs. If someone is offering you 'free' education or property advice, approach with caution. Almost everything has a price. Those enthusiastic 'experts' may receive a kickback for recommending certain property developments or off-the-plan apartments. This sort of advice should be taken with a big grain of salt. It may not be completely independent or represent your best interests.

Always ensure any investment advice you get is independent and in line with your long-term goals.

FRIENDS AND FAMILY ARE NOT INVESTORS

Another disincentive can be that other people in your friendship circles aren't doing it.

Some really inspiring 19- and 20-year-olds who have read *Positively Geared* come to me and say, 'I want to get started — *now*'. It's amazing. They don't have any money but they want to make a start. They want a strategy and to understand what they have to do, but then they also want to go out partying with their friends. Because if they were to say, 'No, I can't afford to go out because I'm saving up to buy a house', there's a good chance their mates would laugh at them, so there's some psychology behind that. I know what it's like to be the only one who was saving instead of going out with my friends from the Con every weekend — and sometimes I did wonder if it was really worth it.

Not only are your friends probably not investing, but maybe even some of your own relatives at the Sunday afternoon barbecue are among the nay-sayers: 'You won't make any money in property!' or 'Why are you buying in *that* location?' or 'The market is about to crash'.

Again, be cautious of who you listen to, and seek out those who are already successful property investors.

When your family are not investors, you need to dig even deeper to back yourself. Most people come from families like mine who didn't get second mortgages because they were afraid to take a risk. That was challenging, as I didn't know where to start.

Even more challenging for potential investors is generational poverty, because it can be difficult to break that chain. If your parents were renting the properties you lived in growing up, and living paycheque to paycheque, and you follow in their footsteps, then your own kids may inherit that mindset, and this relationship with money (or the lack of it) becomes generational.

If you're determined to invest in property and get ahead, but you were brought up to believe money is the root of all evil, then you have to be the one who decides, *I don't want to live the way my parents and grandparents lived. I want to be able to provide better opportunities for my kids. I want to be able to buy a nice home and take my family on a holiday every year — and do other things my parents could never do because we couldn't afford to.*

You need to be able to make these decisions for yourself.

IT ALL COMES BACK TO STRATEGY

To be confident in your investment, you need to make sure you're buying a property that you believe has the fundamentals to grow in value, and you need to make sure that you're buying a property that is within your pre-approved budget. You also need a strategy around whether it should be cashflow-positive right away or whether you're fine with building up to that.

In your due diligence you'll consider all the things that make an investment property great — like location, population growth, amenities and government spending on infrastructure. Check the property's potential growth statistics. Look at how much it's going to cost you, the rent it will likely draw, and the outgoings, such as council and water. Will it be negatively geared, neutral, positively geared or cashflow-positive?

And yes, there is a difference between positively geared and cashflow-positive. A positively geared property is only positive once your tax refund is taken into account. A cashflow-positive property is one that pays you from day one. Is the property still going to be cashflow-positive after all the costs involved have been covered, or is it not quite the right property for you?

You might start by asking yourself, 'Okay, where can I invest that's going to get me the return I'm looking for?' Perhaps you're thinking you should only buy in Sydney or Melbourne, because they continue to enjoy the highest capital growth in the country, but the catch is that those cities' *rental* yields are very low. So, even if on an average income, you *can* buy a property in those markets, the lower rental yields may well prevent you from moving forward to the next property. Rental yield is total rental income divided by the property purchase price and multiplied by 100. A 5.2 per cent yield is considered neutral.

So you need to determine the rental income on the property you're buying and ensure that it's either close to neutral or positively geared (or, better still, cashflow-positive), and you can continue to grow your portfolio because the mortgage is covered by the rent.

A lot of my strategies, like building duplexes, subdivisions and renovations, focus on *adding value* to property, a topic I will go into further in the next chapter.

INVESTING IN A HOME VS BECOMING AN INVESTOR

In chapter 4, we walked through the wish list document that I use to help home buyers understand what they're trying to achieve when looking for a home. If they want to live in Bondi Beach but they've only got $1 million, I'll suggest they consider a suburb that is a more realistic target for them to begin with, pointing out gently, 'Well, you won't find a five-bedroom house you can afford in Bondi, but you'll find it in Campbelltown'.

If they're determined to buy close to Bondi, I introduce them to suburbs nearby where they might be able to afford at least an apartment; it won't be a five-bedroom home, but it might at least keep them close to where they want to live.

We try to guide them based on what they're looking for and to match their goals as closely as possible. We dig deep so we can get a true understanding of what they want. But the insights we derive from the client's wish list are specific to home buyers, not investors. There are more things to think about when buying as a homeowner because it is inevitably an emotional purchase.

As we discussed in chapter 4, if you're a homeowner on a budget, there are more things you may need to compromise on. That's when you have to ask yourself lots of questions. For example, 'Do I mind if it's near a train line or a major flight path?' You might be happy to put up with the aircraft noise because you really want to live in a certain area.

When working with investor clients, I substitute the wish list for our Property Strategy Selection document, in which we plan what each investment property might look like. For example, if they come to us with a $1.2 million borrowing capacity, we may recommend that they begin with a $700 000 property with a 10 per cent deposit, and we'll look at the suburbs available.

Scan the QR code to see the Property Strategy Selection document we use.

Then we look at the time frame. As this will be their first property, and they have the finance pre-approved, we can move forward as soon as we find them the right property.

I'll go into more detail about choosing the right market in the next chapter but, for example, if we decide to purchase in Western Sydney, Newcastle, Central Coast, Geelong or even Brisbane, we'll be confident of capital growth, so that's the strategy we'll focus on. We'll look at cashflow and manufacturing equity as well, we'll also take account of their serviceability, but capital growth will be our main strategy.

NEW INVESTOR MISTAKE #1: NO GROWTH

You need positive cashflow to help pay off your investment loans and raise your serviceability from the banks. However, you can't just rely on getting cashflow-positive properties, because if they don't enjoy growth—if they're worth much the same in 10 years' time as when you bought them—then you'll be no further ahead. It's a mistake many people make.

To avoid getting stuck, strategies include buying in an area with strong capital growth, doing a subdivision or increasing your equity through renovation.

A property might achieve 6 per cent annual growth over a 10-year period. The way cycles work, as we've discussed, you might get 10 or 12 per cent in a couple of those years, while in other years you might achieve only 2 or 3 per cent, but it will usually average out. In a good growth area, you might see 6 per cent growth in your property each year, on average. Now, if you buy a property for $700 000 and you get 6 per cent growth per year over 10 years, your property will be worth $1.3 million.

Now let's say you buy into an area that sees no growth, such as an outback regional area or a one-horse mining town at a time when there's no resources boom. If you saw only 1 per cent annual growth in that property's value, that means after eight years the value of your $700 000 property has risen to only $758 000.

That's why capital growth is so important for investors. Early in my investing career, my own 'big mistake' property in Blackwater, a one-horse mining town, did far worse than that. So do ensure you invest in an area with lots of 'horses'!

DO PROPERTIES IN HIGH-GROWTH AREAS COST MORE?

Of course, properties in high-growth areas nearly always cost more than their equivalents in low-growth areas. That's why you need to balance things out.

Over the past two decades, since I started investing in 2003, probably the biggest change we've seen in Australia's property market is the barrier that now prevents all but those with high incomes or inherited cash to enter the Sydney and Melbourne markets. Many investors today still want to invest in these expensive markets, even though they have neither a big enough deposit saved up nor the borrowing capacity.

I generally advise against investing in property in Sydney at the moment. In fact, if you're at the start of putting together your investment portfolio, just about anywhere *other* than Sydney or Melbourne will be more affordable. You need to look at markets outside of the capitals — but also, to look at strategies for making the most of those properties.

There are many other really good growth areas in major cities such as Newcastle or Wollongong, for example. Or look at other capital cities, such as Brisbane and Adelaide, where property is still relatively cheaper *and* the rental yields are better.

In Newcastle you can find both growth and yield. Although the growth may not be as high as in Sydney, the rental yield will be higher and the up-front costs lower. This better balance is a great opportunity for you to get onto the property ladder.

These days we are seeing a lot of regional markets, such as Orange, Port Macquarie, Albury/Wodonga and Ballarat, really take off. And then there are those coastal areas like Lennox Head, Byron Bay, the Sunshine Coast and, more recently, the Sapphire Coast in southern NSW, which have been great growth areas. I myself have recently purchased two properties on the Sapphire Coast.

CASE STUDY
BUYING YOUR FIRST INVESTMENT PROPERTY

The following case study is based around a hypothetical client named Tony to take the mystery out of the crucial first steps along the pathway to financial freedom. This case study was originally put together for an interview with *Australian Property Investor* magazine.

TONY'S SITUATION

A Sydney-based panelbeater, Tony has recently had some success in trading cryptocurrency and is considering shifting his earnings into a brick-and-mortar investment. He is hesitant about moving into property, though, as he's worried about the unexpected expenses he might accrue in managing a rental.

Tony pays around $1400 a month for the mortgage on his home in Seven Hills, which he purchased in 2012. He has no other major debt commitments. He also has the equivalent of $85 000 in his cryptocurrency portfolio and is willing to use $70 000 of that as a deposit. His annual salary is $83 000. He has obtained pre-approval to borrow $480 000 and he wants a cashflow-positive investment.

What are the best options to ensure Tony's rental property won't leave him out of pocket?

The good news for Tony is that properties at price points below $500 000 generally have better cashflow than their more expensive counterparts.

THE STRATEGY

Firstly, I would advise Tony to seek counsel from an accountant to decide on the structure to set up for this purchase. His home in Seven Hills is in his own name; however, for his first investment property, Tony should consider whether purchasing in a trust would be a better option.

He needs to weigh up the asset protection offered by a trust against the changed tax implications and decide whether he needs to set up a discretionary trust for his family. His accountant will discuss with him whether asset protection is a priority in his line of work as a panelbeater.

Although Tony has his loan pre-approval in place, he will need to sell the equivalent of $70 000 in crypto to raise his deposit before he can start sourcing properties. Actually, he'll have to sell slightly more than $70 000 in crypto, as the proceeds will be subject to CGT because Tony acquired and held his cryptocurrency as an investment.

Without CGT, the numbers for Tony's property's purchase will look like the following:

» He will need to purchase at 90 per cent LVR. Assuming a $400 000 property purchase, this will mean a $40 000 deposit.

(continued)

» If he gets a loan at above 80 per cent, he'll have to pay LMI of $5000 to $10 000.

» Tony will need to allow for stamp duty of $16 000 and $3000 to cover legals and incidentals, including building and pest inspections.

» This takes the total initial funds required to $59 000, leaving him $11 000 as a buffer, for tax, CGT and any repairs or upgrades needed.

» Although Tony's pre-approval is for $480 000, I would recommend he limit the purchase price to $400 000 because of his available deposit of $70 000. This is assuming Tony is employed as a panelbeater. If he is self-employed, it will be harder for him to get a loan at 90 per cent LVR, and he may need a larger deposit, as few banks will lend more than 80 per cent of the purchase price to sole traders.

DUE DILIGENCE

The key to Tony's purchase is to buy a property that is positively geared or, even better, cashflow-positive (before tax), so it won't leave him out of pocket. While cashflow is important in this scenario, growth is also important. So we'll be targeting specific regional areas with good growth drivers and rental yields. It's important that Tony has a cashflow-positive property, as he is already paying $1400 a month from his salary on his home in Seven Hills and he needs to mitigate cashflow risks.

It's important that Tony doesn't get 'maxed out' or he won't be able to buy further investment properties. Buying well below Tony's pre-approved budget, along with having good cashflow, will help him with serviceability for his next property, when he's ready to enter the market again.

For Tony's purchase, I would be advocating the regional north-west NSW town of Armidale, where houses have seen high growth over the past 12 months (at the time of writing), and this growth is trending upwards. The average rental yield in Armidale is 5 per cent and the median house price is $375 000, meaning we should be able to find something for well under Tony's budget. The key is to buy *under the median* in a suburb.

Armidale hosts the University of New England and the town's hospital recently had an $81 million upgrade. It's also a testing ground for the NBN network and one of the NSW Government's 'Evocities'.

There is a shortage of rental properties in Armidale at the moment and rental prices are increasing, which will help ensure that Tony has a property that is easy to rent out and will not cost him. We're looking at buying in an area with a vacancy rate of below 2 per cent.

I would also advise Tony to take out an interest-only loan to ensure his property is cashflow-positive. He may need to refinance it at the end of the interest-free period to ensure he can extend the interest-free terms.

A STEP-BY-STEP GUIDE TO INVESTING IN PROPERTY

If you're ready to start planning your first investment, these are the steps you'll need to take.

STRATEGISE – KNOW YOUR WHY AND CREATE AN INVESTMENT STRATEGY

As I always say, you need a reason to invest and a vehicle that motivates you to stick to your investment strategy. So before you begin to work on your strategy, clearly define your big-picture lifestyle goal. Is it financial freedom? Working for yourself? Semi-retirement? More overseas holidays? Helping underprivileged communities? Once you've crystallised this, you can begin working on your strategy.

Next, determine where, when and what you want to buy. Your goals will inform this decision. For example, you might buy a blue-chip property for long-term growth, or build a duplex for cashflow.

NEW INVESTOR MISTAKE #2: NO STRATEGY

Even in a booming property market, you can't just buy any property and instantly retire. If you're lucky, you may earn some cash in the short term, but it won't get you closer to your ultimate goal.

Having a balanced portfolio is key, and each purchase should be the next step in your long-term strategic plan, enabling you to grow your portfolio.

A strategic investment plan should always be drawn up with the end-goal in mind, and should be reviewed annually as well as after each property purchase. It's also wise to review your plan if there has been a dramatic change in the investing environment.

In the Property Strategy Selection document, there's a section that can track portfolio growth. We use this to see how our client's strategy is working. I also use this document to monitor and grow my own portfolio.

🤝 SECURE FINANCE

Many people are under the impression that you need millions of dollars and a huge borrowing capacity to invest, but this is far from the truth. Getting a mortgage is not always easy, though, so consult a mortgage broker as soon as you can. They will assess your financial position and advise you how banks will see it. As I cover in chapter 3, they'll explain the different types of interest rates, ascertain what loans are likely to best suit your goals and strategy, determine the best lender for your needs, and outline any changes you'll need to make before applying for your home loan of choice.

If you're proceeding on your own, though, you'll need to show lenders who you are, what area you're buying in, what type of property you're buying, the intent behind the purchase and how much you need to borrow. Be sure to also save a strong buffer for costs, as these are easy to underestimate, and saving enough just to cover your deposit will only lead to financial stress.

HOW MUCH DO YOU NEED TO BUY A PROPERTY?

Occasionally I encounter clients with substantial savings in the bank, but with the mindset that they need to keep saving. *We don't have enough yet — we need a 30 per cent deposit before we can buy*. For anyone who's in this position, I'll reiterate that you may well be ready to go to market *now*. In fact, you might be in a position to buy *multiple* properties, and start creating some instant leverage for building a portfolio.

Investing in a property is obviously quite different from buying your own home. Essentially, for an investment property, you just need a 10 per cent deposit (depending on your circumstances and serviceability). That's where the advice of a good mortgage broker is of value. They can look at your situation and determine if you are in the financial position to put down a 10 per cent deposit and borrow the rest.

With that 30 per cent deposit, you might be able to buy a couple of properties and really get a foot on the ladder.

Having sought that advice, you can begin putting in place a strategy that allows you to move forward with confidence.

So how much money do you actually need to get into a property? Well, as an example of getting in on the cheaper side, if you buy in a regional area, and the property costs $400 000, then you really only need a 10 per cent deposit — $40 000 — plus stamp duty and legals.

That said, I don't recommend getting into a property like that unless you're actually going to do something with it. You might do a renovation, or a subdivision that creates separate titles. Or you might build a granny flat in the backyard for cashflow. Because generally you'll see slower growth in most of the regions than in the capital cities.

But buying into a market like that has the great advantage of giving you a foot in the door much sooner than you might otherwise manage.

At the moment, of course, prices are rising in regional areas too. Many of these regions saw higher growth as a result of COVID-19, with families moving away from the cities for lifestyle reasons.

But what if you have managed to save a much higher deposit and therefore have a much higher borrowing capacity? I advise against spending it all on one property, putting all your eggs in one basket. Speak to an expert — an independent buyer's agent or property adviser. Discuss diversifying across a couple of properties — one in Victoria and one in NSW, for example. That will really help you get ahead.

🤝 HIRE YOUR DREAM TEAM

As well as your buyer's agent, mortgage broker, accountant, and solicitor or conveyancer, your dream team might include a financial planner, a building and pest inspector, a quantity surveyor, an architect, a property manager and an insurance representative, as well as multiple building contractors, depending on your strategy.

Once you find reliable professionals, you'll probably want to use their services on multiple projects spanning many years as you build your investment property portfolio.

Do your own due diligence on the property you want to buy, but once you've bought it, you can leave it to the professionals to look after it while you move on. If you're building a duplex, for example, the builders will take on the responsibility of construction.

🤝 FIND A SUITABLE INVESTMENT PROPERTY

Less than 5 per cent of available properties are 'investment grade'. So how do you find a good property in a region that's ripe for growth? You should be able to narrow your search by applying the property trifecta: instant equity, cashflow and growth.

To achieve this, shortlist properties based on the following factors:

- solid regional growth drivers
- several different industries in the area
- increased government spending in the area
- good transport links

- low local unemployment rate
- low property vacancy rate
- proximity to childcare and educational facilities
- in a school catchment zone
- in a quiet street
- a good floorplan
- not in a flood zone
- not close to a major flight path.

Searching and doing your due diligence takes time, so you need to be patient.

NEW INVESTOR MISTAKE #3: BUYING CLOSE TO HOME

I see this happen a lot. A great area to live in isn't necessarily a great place to invest. Buying close to home may make it an emotional purchase that's not aligned with your long-term strategy.

Never buy an investment property based on emotion. Once emotion is in the picture, risks can be overlooked, your due diligence is less thorough, and your market research less extensive. Always do thorough research to determine the market that best suits your specific goal. That way, you'll know you're on the right path to creating a solid investment portfolio.

NEW INVESTOR MISTAKE #4: NOT ENOUGH RESEARCH

I cannot emphasise enough how important it is to do your research on the property. For example, never avoid doing a building and pest inspection to save money. This crucial step should always be

(continued)

budgeted into your purchase costs. A professional inspection can save you from buying a property that has underlying structural issues or termite damage requiring costly repairs.

Conducting extensive research on the area is also crucial. Look at growth trends, comparable rentals and sales, and the investing environment to ensure you're purchasing the most suitable property for your portfolio.

Understanding the economic drivers of an area is important, as is weighing up the benefits and risks of each option. Purchasing the wrong property can cost you thousands and stop your portfolio growth in its tracks!

FROM SIGNING TO SETTLING

Once you've found your property, placed a bid and had it accepted (or you've been the successful bidder at auction), contracts between you and the vendor are signed and exchanged.

Take note of any special conditions, disclosures and insurance in your contract of sale. It's also important to know what can be negotiated in the contract. This may include the cooling-off period, the settlement period, the deposit amount, and fittings and fixtures. Ensure that you send a copy of the contract to your lender if you are getting finance.

On settlement day, all representatives of the parties, including financiers, communicate with each other to exchange legal documents.

NEGOTIATING PRICE

Whether or not you're using a buyer's agent, you need to be realistic about what the market's doing, as this will give you a good idea about what your offer on a property should be.

Sometimes people will ask me, 'Can you get it at 20 per cent below market value?' Just because I'm a buyer's agent doesn't mean that's going to happen. Legally, agents are expected to take *any* offer to the vendor, but I know many who won't do so if it's a ridiculous offer. I can't blame them.

For a property advertised at $3 million, offering the vendor $2 million is not realistic. The agent won't go to the vendor and say, 'Well, we've got an offer for you — and it's a third less than your asking price'.

To my mind, it's got to be a fair offer. I assess the fair market value of that property and put in a reasonable offer, knowing the vendor's agent will come back with a counteroffer and we'll go from there. But if I put in a ridiculously low offer, they won't take me seriously — and that's not good for my credibility. Keep that in mind when negotiating, because even if you don't succeed on that property, you might want to buy another one through that agent down the track.

I always give our clients sound, realistic advice on what their offer should be for a property, rather than simply agreeing with what the client *thinks* they should be paying.

AUCTION VS PRIVATE TREATY

I've already noted that I really like the auction process because it's transparent. People say, 'Oh, you have to pay too much at auction', but *true market value is what the market will pay on the day*. Some clients come to me after missing out at auctions for months, and they're tearing their hair out. But most often they're looking at the wrong properties and have the wrong expectations, because they don't know the market well enough.

So, for example, if you've got a million-dollar budget and you start by looking at properties with price guides of a million dollars, you're looking at the wrong properties, because while those properties aren't under-quoted (because it's illegal to under-quote), that's only a base price guide. The property is more likely to sell for $1.2 million, $1.3 million or more in the current market. Prospective buyers really need to understand that.

One reason I have a really good record of success at auctions is that I know the markets, and I can advise and educate our clients accordingly. So if they have a million-dollar budget, we'll actually bring them back a bit and say, 'You should be looking at this property; it has two bedrooms instead of three and the price guide is $750 000, so we should be able to get this and stay within your budget'.

To a great extent, success at auctions is about managing people's expectations. This is why in most cases I recommend using a professional bidder or buyer's agent to attend auctions on your behalf.

🤝 BECOMING A LANDLORD

It's important to understand your responsibilities as a landlord to avoid costly mistakes, maximise your returns and protect your investment. This includes understanding relevant legislation set out by the state or territory of the area in which you're buying. It also means appointing a property manager, and doing your homework around that. Don't just go with the cheapest or biggest agency.

When assessing prospective tenants, screen them thoroughly by running credit checks, assessing their employment and rental history, and contacting their referees. Once the lease is signed, remember to budget for upkeep on the property. You need to maintain your investment.

LANDLORD INSURANCE

While it's not compulsory, like your building insurance, landlord insurance is an absolute must-have. It protects your income and safeguards you against theft and accidental damage to the contents of your investment property.

Some big insurance companies offer landlord insurance policies, but I recommend seeking advice from your property manager or our service. Take the time to read the fine print, as some policies aren't as good as they sound. Some, for example, exclude claims for loss of rent if your tenant is not on a fixed lease agreement.

 **DREAM TEAM PROPERTY MANAGERS**

I outsource every single property in my portfolio to property managers. A good property manager is worth their weight in gold, even though their commission comes out of your rental income.

SEARCHING FOR A PROPERTY MANAGER

» Look locally—local knowledge is crucial.

» Do your research.

» Rely on word of mouth.

» Find out what services they offer.

» Compare how quickly they respond to calls and emails.

» Ask questions.

» Count the cost.

Most of my properties are pretty much 'set and forget'. So, although I don't recommend that you set and forget when it comes to your bank loan, the property itself should be completely looked after once purchased. This is why it's important to find a good property manager. They take care of finding tenants and making sure you get your rent. They conduct inspections and deal with any repairs on the property. You shouldn't have to worry about things like that because your time is taken up with work, family or building your property portfolio.

 CASE STUDY
FIRST-TIME INVESTOR ON HER WAY TO FINANCIAL FREEDOM

Lucy was referred to us by a mortgage broker we know. She was keen to set herself up for the future, but she didn't know where to start. Lucy's budget was a maximum of $400 000.

(continued)

THE STRATEGY

Lucy, in her thirties, decided she wanted to set herself up to achieve financial freedom after watching her parents doing it tough and having to rely on the pension for their retirement, which they could barely enjoy because of low cashflow.

Lucy came to us to discuss her options. After reviewing her situation and goals, we decided on the strategy of finding her a high-yielding property with good long-term growth potential. We also concentrated on properties where Lucy could add value through a cosmetic renovation, which would allow her to create instant equity instead of just relying on the natural growth of the market. This would accelerate the process of building her portfolio.

Lucy's limited budget meant we had to look outside of Sydney. We focused the search on some good regional towns we were familiar with in both south east Queensland and regional NSW. This would allow Lucy to enjoy excellent cashflow while gaining good growth and equity in the property, without affecting her serviceability for the next purchase.

THE CHALLENGES

During our search, property prices continued to rise, as they had been doing for many years in these regions: they'd gained 20 per cent in the previous three years alone. To avoid paying too much, I knew it was important to make decisions based purely on research and data rather than emotion.

After inspecting a number of properties and presenting them to Lucy for comparison, we advised her on which property would make the best investment for her in the short and long term. It was a three-bedroom, two-bathroom house with multiple living areas on a large corner block in the central west region of NSW. We provided full property profile reports, with data on the property, the town, demographics, population, jobs growth and infrastructure.

(continued).

NEGOTIATIONS AND ACQUISITION

Lucy was thrilled with this standout property. It was time to negotiate. Knowing it was going to be a great first investment for Lucy, setting the foundations of her property portfolio, with a further 8 to 10 per cent growth expected in the next 12 months, we were keen to secure this deal.

The property had been on the market for a little while; initially, the vendor had been asking for $409 000, so we were going to have to work hard to get this down to a price we were comfortable with and make sure Lucy wasn't overpaying.

We submitted an offer and the agent came back to us to say the vendor had now decided to hold onto the property and put a tenant in. We knew we had to be persistent to get the vendor to change their mind, and that meant giving them an attractive incentive in the form of a higher deposit and shorter settlement terms.

THE RESULT

The next email came through with 'Congratulations...'! We were relieved that our hard work and persistence had paid off. Lucy was so happy to hear that our offer of $350 000 had been accepted. It was an incredible result.

We helped Lucy organise a building and pest inspection, provided guidance on getting her formal finance approval, booked in the valuation and put her in touch with an exceptional property manager. As we were approaching settlement, we asked the property manager to start marketing the property for rent. After the first open house, one week before settlement, a tenant was secured, which guaranteed Lucy an income as soon as she collected the keys.

The lesson here is how important it is to choose the right property to suit the local demographics, which will ensure it's in high demand and reduce any vacancy periods.

(continued)

THE NUMBERS

Property purchase price:	$350 000
Stamp duty:	$10 957
Legals:	$1800
Building and pest inspection:	$660
TOTAL PURCHASE COSTS:	**$363 417**
Rent per week:	$490
Yield:	7.28%

CHAPTER 7

CREATE YOUR OWN EQUITY

Mind-blowing profit through property advancement

Growth is the cornerstone of everything you need to do as a property investor. Manufacturing growth means creating instant equity in a property. If you do this, rather than waiting for growth, you can control the growth in your property and thereby 'control the market'. It is a much-overlooked topic that is very close to my heart.

Equity in a property is the difference between its market value — based on the bank valuation — and how much you owe on the property. If you have, say, a $400 000 loan on the property and the bank values the property at $600 000, then you have $200 000 in equity. If you do something to that property to raise the equity — for example, a renovation — and the bank revalues it at $700 000, then you've created an extra $100 000 in equity, for an overall total of $300 000 in equity.

Manufacturing equity simply means doing something that increases the value of a property and makes the bank revalue the property at a higher amount, which is how you know you've actually raised your equity in that property. So you can do the work — a substantial renovation, for example — and assume you've raised the equity as a result, but you won't know this for sure until the bank's valuation or until you sell the property. If you sell, the equity you gain becomes your profit, and you won't need that bank valuation (although the new buyer will need one if obtaining finance).

CAPITAL GROWTH VS MANUFACTURED GROWTH

Most people buy property and wait for capital growth over time. They hope the market will continue to rise over a few years, increasing their property's value. Manufacturing growth means you yourself control the equity in the property.

I'll go into reading the markets in chapter 9, but for now you need to understand that manufacturing equity can help investors to navigate challenging markets where they may not get as much organic capital growth as other areas. It enables them to create equity quickly (though not overnight). Renovation and development are two ways of accomplishing this.

This is important to me because when I first started investing I adopted this 'buy and wait' strategy. I was buying and praying, rather than buying with a strategy. My first three or four properties didn't see much growth, even though I bought them in what were good locations at the time.

One reason for this was that I was buying at the wrong time in the cycle. I bought them after the Sydney 2000 Olympics, so the market had just boomed and was starting to decline. I thought, *I'm doing the right thing here, I'm getting into the market, in good locations* — yet I fell into a lot of debt because I was negatively geared. And that's when things started to change for me, because I started to think about manufacturing growth, and about trying to control my own destiny in the market rather than just doing what everyone else does.

We can't control the amount of growth a property will see or when it will happen, but we all try to buy in markets where we expect growth.

As with all investment properties, we buy where the population is rising, where there's new infrastructure or evidence of government spending, where people want to live and there are low vacancy rates — we cover all these kinds of aspects when doing our due diligence. Other people try to buy in hot spots, which is a strategy I don't really believe in. None of these things guarantee the amount of growth you want.

LEVERAGING YOUR INVESTMENTS

To move forward quickly, you need to be able to control the growth in your own properties yourself, and another thing you should be doing when building a portfolio is leveraging off your investments.

If you buy a property and then wait for growth that doesn't happen, you risk getting stuck. That's why most property investors never get past one or two properties. They're buying the wrong property in the wrong location.

The worst thing you can do is buy a property then, five or 10 years later, find it hasn't improved much in value since you bought it. But if you buy a property and actually do something with it, and six or 12 months later you've added some value to that property, then you've increased your equity and the rental yield so you'll be in a better position without the wait.

You can also *leverage the equity* to get yourself into another property deal. So instead of passively waiting perhaps five years to get into another property, or having to save up for several years to get enough for another deposit, you can get into another property six or 12 months later, because you've increased your equity very quickly. You can then repeat the process and build a portfolio much faster.

This is good, as *you* have controlled when the growth happens rather than waiting for six or 10 years to get the growth. It often comes down to buying in the right location, because if your property doesn't increase in value in 10 years, then you bought in the wrong location and your due diligence was wrong in the first place.

I like manufacturing growth as it gives me more control over my investments. It's also good for flipping, as you can raise the property's value, then sell quickly. You can do the same with your home, of course. It's what I did with my homes in Ingleburn and Lewisham, and I'll tell you more about that in chapter 8.

TIMING THE MARKET FOR EXTRA GROWTH

Timing the market isn't that important for manufacturing growth, because you can manufacture growth no matter what the market is doing. That's the point of the strategy. But you can't really focus on market timing *and* create equity at the same time, as you risk lapsing into analysis paralysis. *Is this market going to grow or not? Maybe I should wait.* Manufacturing growth is about *not* having to wait for the market. It's about *creating growth* at any point in the cycle, and not relying on what the market's doing now or what it's *going* to do.

WILL MANUFACTURING EQUITY WORK FOR EVERY PROPERTY?

An investor might be holding a property that hasn't done much over the years; it might even have gone backwards in value. They're wondering whether to keep it or consider selling it at a loss. In this situation, forcing some value into that property might help them get out at less of a loss.

This doesn't mean that every time you buy a property you should be looking for something really rundown that you can improve through a renovation. That strategy is not for everyone. You don't need to create quick equity with every property you buy, but it's certainly worth identifying where it's an option, particularly if you're buying in a market not known for high growth. This can be the case if you're on a lower budget and buying a cheaper regional property or chasing cashflow. Again, it comes down to strategy.

People who buy in the Sydney and Melbourne markets are always going to do relatively well. But outside Sydney and Melbourne, many markets either fluctuate more than the big two or experience less growth overall.

If you're investing in one of the *other* capital cities — or in a regional area — I recommend looking into how you could manufacture equity in the property you buy, rather than just buying and holding.

REGIONAL MARKET STRATEGY

Manufacturing growth is a good way to create a really solid foundation, particularly when you're buying outside of the stronger metropolitan markets, because if you buy into a country area you could be in for an even longer wait for substantial growth. This strategy is really important if you're in an area that doesn't have a lot of growth and you want to build up a portfolio.

The best part of this strategy is that if you buy into a regional area where prices are lower, even with a small deposit you can manufacture some growth, and you can then use that equity to leverage into other, perhaps better markets. For example, you might buy into a regional area by spending $400 000 to $450 000 on a property, then do a cosmetic renovation or a subdivision, forcing some equity into your portfolio. Then rinse and repeat.

WHY I STARTED MANUFACTURING EQUITY

The biggest hurdle for me when I first stepped onto the property ladder was raising the capital for a deposit. As I've noted, after I bought my first property, the Rockdale unit, it was quite a while before I bought my second.

That was partly because at the time I hadn't imagined I was going to become a serious property investor, so I didn't jump into the market really quickly. I bought one property, then a few years later I bought another. When I bought the second property, I'd been saving money along the way and had built up some equity in my first property.

The second property, my home at Ingleburn in south-west Sydney, cost me only $260 000. It needed a bit of renovation so I did some work on the kitchen, a complete paint job and a little basic cosmetic reno stuff.

I moved out of Rockdale and into Ingleburn, then did some work on the Rockdale property and turned it into an investment.

By the time I bought my third property, saving money was proving difficult. Working in a nine-to-five job for a modest income, I wasn't saving a lot of money and couldn't afford blue-chip properties. So for me it was about investing in the cheaper outer suburbs and regional towns.

I was also trying to minimise the deposit I had to pay. When I was building my portfolio I aimed for a 10 per cent deposit even if I actually had a bit more, because the little left over could then be put towards a renovation to manufacture equity so I could get into my next property. Back in those days, sometimes you could pay a 5 per cent deposit. These days, banks' lending criteria often require a deposit of 20 per cent, although you can still do 10 per cent if your serviceability allows it.

As you know, the big change for me came when I did my first duplex build. That was a different type of manufacturing equity that really got my portfolio going. I found that the equity I created by building my first duplex was twice as much as I then earned from a whole year as a teacher, and I realised if I kept doing that I could one day achieve my goal of financial security.

GROWTH STRATEGIES

LLOYD'S STRATEGY

It's all about investing strategically and creating a road map setting out how you'll achieve your goals.

As I often say, 'Everything always comes back to strategy'. There are many different ways you can look at buying a property — depending on your stage of life, how much money you have, and whether you want to *buy and hold* or *buy, increase equity and sell quickly*. All of these perspectives, while separate, have significant crossover.

There are also a lot of variables involved in determining how far you need to go to manufacture growth. The state and region you're buying in are going to affect what due diligence you can do before buying, and when you'll look to manufacturing growth in that property down the track, depending on your financial goal.

If you're planning to manufacture equity in a property, you've got to be clear about your reason for doing so. Some investors will buy a property that needs some work, but they don't really need the equity straight away, so they put off this work. Others may not be looking for equity but want to increase the rental income to improve cashflow. But if your strategy is to buy a property then have that property help you get into another property in six or 12 months' time, I'd advise you to look at increasing the equity on that property as soon as possible after you buy it.

Scan the QR code for a personalised property strategy selection table.

🏠 STRATEGY: RENOVATION FOR GROWTH

If you're going to do a renovation, you need to make sure you're buying into an area where there's quite a lot of difference in sales prices between unrenovated and renovated properties. So if you buy an old four-bedroom fibro home and up the street there are other similar fibro homes that have been renovated, those homes need to be selling for a fair bit more than similar, unrenovated ones. If there's not much difference in value between the two, then you know you'll be overcapitalising if you go and do a substantial renovation. It's probably not the right area for a renovation. You need to look at that and crunch some numbers.

Before I go unconditional on a contract, I always get tradies to come in and give me some quotes on how much their work would cost. Depending on which state you're buying in, this could be either during the cooling-off period or within the finance clause period. If you're in Queensland, for example, you have a 21-day finance clause there so you've got a bit of extra time in which to get those sorts of things done. Make sure you're getting those quotes so you know what you're up for.

My rule of thumb when doing renovations is to aim to add three dollars of value for every dollar I spend. So if you're going to spend $20 000 on a renovation, you should be able to make $60 000 in equity from it. If you can't get those numbers, then the renovation is probably not a good idea.

You need to know the costings around what you plan to do, and what areas you're going to spend your renovation money on. Sometimes the property will just need a bit of paint work or floor coverings or window coverings, which won't cost you much at all. Maybe just updating the kitchen and bathroom will add a lot of equity. Keep in mind the demographics of that area, and what is likely to appeal to people in that demographic. I'll tell you all about this in the next chapter.

STRATEGY: SUBDIVISION AND DUPLEXES

One way of manufacturing equity that I often use is to buy a house on a large block of land, subdivide that land using a Torrens title subdivision, then build a house or a duplex in the backyard. By building a duplex, you effectively turn one property into three properties, and you can either rent them all or sell one, two or all three of them.

A duplex can be Strata titled on top of the Torrens title subdivision you did on the block. So you have effectively created three separate properties, each with its own title and valuation, from what was just one property when you purchased it.

Sometimes you might buy a property like that even though you can't afford to build the duplex right away, knowing it has the potential to be developed down the track. That's the real winner in a lot of the stuff I do. When buying a property, I don't need to go through the whole development process right away. It's a matter of recognising its potential.

And even without doing anything to it, you can still sell it for a premium if you need to, as the property still has that potential.

A simpler process is to do a straight-out duplex build, as illustrated in the case studies in earlier chapters. You can do this as a knockdown and rebuild, or just find some vacant land and build a duplex on it. On completion, you subdivide the property so you've got two units on two separate titles. The construction of a duplex typically takes six to eight months, plus the time it takes to get council approval.

Again, the key is making sure you're building for less than you can sell it for afterwards. If you can do the whole project for, say, $900 000 and you know that each unit is going to sell for $550 000, that's a total of $1 100 000, so you will have created $200 000 in equity. The point is you've got to do your numbers and your feasibility research before you go all in.

My first development was a big learning curve for me. I had a few issues with the local council and was working with a builder for the first time — it was all new to me. But the results I got in the end were just so much better than I was expecting, which was a huge relief.

It was 2012, and I bought a corner block in the best part of Armidale, in NSW's Northern Tablelands, for $159 000, and I built a duplex on it. The whole development project, including construction, council costs, stamp duty and legals, came to $629 000. When it was completed I had it subdivided, and the two separate properties were valued at $380 000 and $390 000. This left me with $141 000 in equity.

STRATEGY: HIGH-GROWTH AREAS

There's always a solution that allows you to move forward, whether you've got $300 000 or $2 million to spend on property. But some markets offer *better* solutions. As always, it comes down to strategy.

People who are looking for high-growth areas should understand that at any given time there are many different price points and locations that will enable you to achieve higher manufactured growth within a shorter time.

When building or developing property, I always target areas where I feel there's going to be a lot of organic growth, because although sometimes I'll build and sell, I might want to keep the property, adding it to my portfolio. So a key is to buy into an area where you expect long-term growth as well.

I talk a lot about the property trifecta: instant equity, cashflow and growth. The key to good investment is looking for properties with the potential to deliver all three.

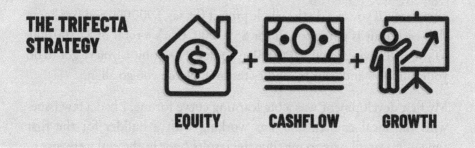

THE TRIFECTA STRATEGY

EQUITY   CASHFLOW   GROWTH

It's well known that the higher the growth, the lower the rental yield, and vice versa. If you get into a high-cashflow market, you'll likely see a bit less growth — and quite often, a lot less growth. Sydney is the lowest-yielding market in the country for that reason.

One way to mitigate that problem is to find a dual-income property in Sydney, such as a house with a granny flat. That certainly helps solve the cashflow problem, although the price point will obviously be a barrier for some investors.

For those on a lower budget, the Central Coast is another good market for these types of dual-income properties. I profile the Central Coast in chapter 9.

Sometimes you may be holding high-growth or blue-chip properties in capital cities but need to complement them with really good cashflow. In that case, getting something outside a capital city with a really good rental yield but not as much growth may be a good strategy. There are many markets outside the capital cities that experience good growth, and you can still buy property in these markets at affordable prices.

Again, it comes down to what you're looking to achieve and how that property will work within your portfolio. That's why it's important to know what you're trying to achieve with each property.

FROM NEGATIVE TO POSITIVE CASHFLOW

I owned four or five properties before I built my first duplex. With these early properties, I wasn't really getting anywhere because there wasn't much growth happening. I was fairly cashflow-negative, too.

It's important for investors to understand how something can work to help get them out of a difficult situation. They may have bought the wrong properties in the wrong locations, and now they're being burned. Quite often there's a reason for that. I've worked with people who have bought properties in places like Gladstone or Mackay in Queensland, towns that are too reliant on the resources sector, which has sometimes resulted in a lack of growth and even market collapse. There's always a reason behind what's happened. If you buy well-located properties and the fundamentals are right, you're going to do better. It's a matter of really understanding what you're doing.

You can also find a property that will help get you *out* of that situation, as long as you understand how it's going to work for you. If you're going to manufacture growth through a renovation or a duplex build, for example, you need to build your confidence and knowledge around that.

Look at the feasibility, how the numbers work, how much it will cost to build, and what sales in the area are like. And if the sales are higher per individual unit than you're building them for, you can take some comfort that your strategy will work. If you've had some bad luck in the past, it just takes a bit of confidence to get all that done.

Working with our clients, we always look at where they are now and what might be the best next step for them to take to move forward. Some may be maxed out with, say, seven or eight properties, but with a really negative cashflow. If they have eight properties and they're losing $1000 a week and facing massive debt, the banks usually won't allow them to borrow any more. So we need to have a conversation about how they can move forward from there.

One option would be to sell the properties that are not performing very well, but that would take time, so we need to look at the long term. Sometimes they are keen to move forward and do a duplex, but that might not be possible just yet. First we need to untangle the situation they're in. That may mean taking three or four months to sell two or three of their existing properties, then getting their finance in order before looking to the next deal.

We need to have those tough conversations and look at those long-term goals. This is why our clients need to share what they're looking to achieve over the next 10, 15 or 20 years. They may have all these properties and all these goals, but it hasn't worked for them so far. How can we reach those goals? Focusing on the long term, three to six months to untangle things is nothing, particularly when we're looking at properties that can provide a fair amount of equity and good cashflow, which can quickly turn things around.

CASE STUDY
FROM $500 000 TO $1.5 MILLION IN PROFIT IN FOUR DEALS

One of my clients, Tom, is an Australian living in the United States. Tom found out about me through the media and approached me to discuss my strategies and how I might be able to help him do some investing in Australia.

THE CHALLENGE

As you know, when someone comes to us, our first priority—apart from the usual discussion about their goals and starting to formulate a strategy—is finance. That's because we can't really do anything without understanding how much they are able to borrow.

As an expat, Tom found that getting a loan was difficult, and he was struggling. He was using his own Australian bank because he needed the loan to be in Australian dollars.

I recommended a broker, but even the broker couldn't find a solution. If he had been living in Australia, he could have got a loan for up to 90 per cent of the purchase price, but an expat can only borrow up to 60 or 70 per cent. So you need a big chunk of equity to put down, which makes it much more expensive to do a deal.

THE SOLUTION

Tom consulted a couple of other brokers, and finally we managed to get him some finance. With a borrowing capacity of about $500 000, he ended up purchasing a property in regional NSW.

It was a house on a large block, and Tom did a one-into-three subdivision. So suddenly he had turned one block of land into three. He kept the front house and is renting it out, then he built another house behind the original one. And he had a third block of land behind the original. By selling both the vacant land and the second house, he managed to make a substantial profit. And he still has the original house.

THE NUMBERS

Property purchase price:	$450 000
Stamp duty:	$15 457
Legals:	$1550
Building and pest inspection:	$660
TOTAL PURCHASE COSTS:	**$467 667**

(continued)

Subdivision costs*:	$55 000
Construction of new home:	$330 000
TOTAL PURCHASE AND DEVELOPMENT COSTS:	**$852 667**
New value of existing house (on smaller block):	$390 000
Rental on existing house:	$480 per week
Sale of new house:	$660 000
Sale of vacant block:	$360 000
TOTAL SALES:	**$1 020 000**
TOTAL PROFIT:	**$167 333 plus $24 960 annual rental income**

* Mostly water and electrical connection fees paid to council, with some going to the surveyor for carrying out the work and preparing the subdivision documentation.

The profit Tom made from this project was enough to enable him to take on another, bigger project. Although his borrowing capacity was still limited to around $600 000 for the next deal, Tom now had a lot more cash to put towards it. He ended up deciding to do a duplex development, and we found him a site to build it on.

Tom walked away with $250 000 in profit from that one. This let him turn his next project into a million-dollar investment. Then he repeated that process and did another duplex after his second deal. Now he's planning a townhouse development.

This townhouse property is on the NSW Central Coast, where the block of land itself was a lot more expensive than his previous properties. Tom is building four townhouses on that block. For this deal he has teamed up with two other investors, and they had a solicitor draw up a joint venture contract. Once that's complete, he stands to make about $1.5 million in profit.

In under five years Tom has gone from being able to afford only one very small acquisition in a regional town to completing a pricey townhouse development. He has achieved that by making successful deals every step of the way.

CHAPTER 8

RENOVATE RIGHT

The do's and 'maybe nots' of renovation

Renovating a property to add value, then either selling it or keeping it in your portfolio, is a strategy that can build wealth and increase the strength of your asset base. In this chapter, I'll outline the best way to generate wealth through renovation, and ensure you get the top dollar for your upgraded property.

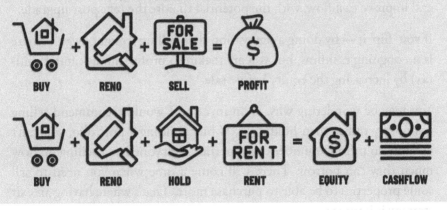

I'm not talking about buying a $2 million property and turning it into a $3.5 million property, the way you've seen it on TV shows like *The Block*. A renovation strategy can be used by people just starting out who want to be active investors and force equity into their properties rather than waiting for market growth.

In a competitive market, a cosmetic renovation can be a quick solution to ensuring you gain maximum interest in your property from prospective buyers or tenants. If you can make your property stand out from the rest, you'll attract more attention and perhaps have more potential buyers or renters competing for it, which will push up the sale price — and maybe the rent too. If you're selling, the increased rent won't affect you but will probably appeal to an investor. But not all renovations are created equal. It needs to be the right one.

SELLING OR HOLDING

Renovating really works for people who are looking to add value to a property and grow their wealth. It's a strategy some people adopt over and over again — 'rinse and repeat'.

The two main growth-building strategies relating to renovation are *selling* and *holding*. Each requires a specific approach and will have a different outcome.

By updating and keeping the property, you manufacture increased equity and improve cashflow, with the potential to raise the rent post-upgrade.

If you 'flip' it — by doing a renovation then selling straight away — there is no ongoing cashflow, but you are making a profit (minus capital gains tax) by increasing the equity before sale.

You may be wondering why, as an investor, I would recommend selling a property rather than holding it. While building a portfolio, you can't just buy an infinite number of properties. Everyone has a ceiling on how much they can borrow. There will come a time when you need to sell some properties to be able to purchase more. That's where having an exit strategy is important.

STARTING A PORTFOLIO THROUGH RENOVATION

The way to begin is to buy, for example, a $400 000 property, do a renovation and sell it for about $500 000, so you've made a decent profit.

That's your bread and butter at this level, and something I have done a few times.

Renovation strategies are a great way for you to add value while working towards your financial and lifestyle goals. For example, if you have $90 000 in the bank when you buy a property and your deposit is $40 000 plus stamp duty and legal fees, you can use what's left over to bring the property up to scratch. But you do need to keep a buffer, so don't spend *all* your money on the project.

By renovating your property you're adding equity that can go towards buying another property. By repeating this process, you can build your way up to a significant portfolio without waiting for organic growth in the market.

Renovation not only increases the value of your property but boosts your cashflow by allowing you to increase the rent. If you buy a property that's renting for $300 a week, but a renovation allows you to increase the rent to $360 a week, that's more money in your pocket. That's an important outcome if you're planning to hold the property to build a portfolio.

TIPS FOR A SUCCESSFUL RENOVATION

To gain an adequate return from a renovation, you need to make sure to get it done in a short amount of time. Ideally, you should have a plan in place so you can get the whole renovation done in four or five weeks, depending on its scope.

This is why it's probably a bad move to decide to do it yourself by going up on weekends for the next six months, because then you're not taking money out of it; you're just putting money into it! Living in the property can certainly save you money, but it really depends on your strategy. Again, you might only work on it on weekends and it might take six months to complete the job. You need to plan what you've got to do and then *get it done*.

FIND YOUR MOTIVATION

To keep things moving, first define your strategy, because therein lies your motivation.

With an investment property, you're more motivated to get the work done quickly because it's a business. You don't want it sitting vacant for six months while not bringing in rent. Remember, it's going to bring in more money once it's done.

If you're flipping to increase the value of a property before selling it, you'll also be motivated to renovate fast so you can put it on the market as soon as possible.

From an investing perspective, renovating your own home to increase and access the equity is much more personal and emotive than numbers on a spreadsheet. That said, you can still set a goal to finish the renovations within a certain time frame — then get a valuer in to assess how much you have increased the equity in your home, ready for investment.

RENOVATE FOR THE MARKET

As an investor and a buyer's agent, I need to know what others are looking for in a property. These are the kinds of things you should consider if you're looking to maximise your equity and returns.

YOUNG PROFESSIONALS

Professionals without children will pay a premium if you install:

- floating or hardwood floors
- a designer kitchen with 900 mm appliances and downlights
- an ensuite for the main bedroom with unique tapware and a shower recess.

FAMILIES WITH YOUNG KIDS

This is about creating that great Australian lifestyle, which means including in the renovation:

- a living area that flows out onto a rear yard for easy access
- secure boundary fencing to safely contain kids and pets
- a cubby house or tree house
- a master bedroom for the parents with walk-in robe and ensuite

- a standalone bath
- a second bathroom or ensuite, if there's only one
- a chef's kitchen, with 900 mm or 1200 mm state-of-the-art appliances
- a 'teenager retreat' for older kids in a downstairs room or the attic, depending on the design of the house.

BLENDED FAMILIES

Dual-income properties — a big home with a separate studio or granny flat; a double-storey duplex; or a single-storey duplex with two separate dwellings divided by a common wall — are a great source of income. You can live in one and rent out the other for additional cashflow, which really helps pay off that mortgage.

They are also usually flexible enough to accommodate blended families. You can put your in-laws or your adult kids and grandkids in one. There are plenty of options and opportunities. I love, and highly recommend, doing dual-income properties.

DOWNSIZERS AND RETIREES

Downsizers usually prefer single-level properties for easier access. This may mean creating paths and removing any small stairs or steps. Areas that are not solid to walk on, such as loose tiles or pavers, must be repaired before anything else. A secure garage with a direct entrance to the main house is ideal.

CREATING EXTRA OFFICE SPACE

Since the COVID-19 pandemic we have seen an increasing trend towards people working from home, which has become a business norm for many big corporations. I believe we are going to see that trend continue and quite possibly become permanent. So it's worthwhile to cater for people who work from home, with at least one designated, functional office space, if not a separate room.

TO DIY OR NOT TO DIY

How much you DIY comes down to cost, time and whether they are major structural renovations. The more renovations you do yourself, the more time they will take but the less they're going to cost, which means more equity in the end. Work out what you can take on yourself. Obviously this will depend on your skillset, your inclination and how much time you have available.

Some people choose to do their own renovations because they enjoy the work. If you're capable of doing it and have the skills needed, I recommend you take it on. It might cost you $5000 to get someone to paint your house, for example, but if you just buy the paint, which might cost you $500 to $800, depending on the size of your house, and do it yourself, that's more than $4000 in equity you've created.

FIRST-TIME RENOVATORS

There are definitely things you can DIY if you're on a budget. However, those new to renovating need to be mindful of what they can actually manage on their own. There are certain tasks you cannot do for safety reasons, such as anything electrical, and I don't recommend you do any plumbing work unless you're properly trained.

Most people can put on new door handles and lay floating floorboards themselves, and you should be able to get around a bit of painting. That said, you don't want to make your house look like it's been worked on by an amateur. So, unless you can do a good job, don't do it yourself.

MY FIRST RENOVATION: INGLEBURN

It was 2007 and I was looking at lots of properties in the Campbelltown area of Sydney. I was buying a home to move into, which would later become an investment.

I found a three-bedroom property in Ingleburn and absolutely fell in love with the kitchen. It had beautiful 40 mm Caesarstone benchtops, state-of-the-art Miele oven and cooktops, and a nice red splashback. Everything was fantastic. Checking the receipts the previous owners had left behind, I discovered it was a $25 000 kitchen, which was expensive back then. That was the *only* stunning part of the place, though; the rest was less than fantastic.

So I bought it for $260 000 with a 10 per cent deposit. As soon as I got the keys, I moved in and did a bit of work on it. I did get a couple of quotes for painting, but at around $3000. I had an extremely limited budget and was really just beginning to grow my portfolio, my friend Steve and I ended up painting the whole joint. I spent about $280 on the paint. Then we updated the bathroom cabinetry and put on better handles and shower tapware. Some of the floorboards were damaged or missing, so I replaced those. I also replaced the window coverings and the front door to give the property a more appealing entrance. I didn't really do much to the front or the back. The front garden didn't look particularly inspiring, and in hindsight I should have done more with the landscaping.

I was never going to stay in Ingleburn forever, but I wanted to live there for a couple of years and then list it as an investment property. I've always liked to live in new properties, though — like my Rockdale unit, which I bought brand new. Ingleburn was an older property that I wanted to modernise. I knew it would immediately add about $50 000 in value, and although I was living in it at the time, there would be equity there if I wanted to refinance. Of course, when I did rent it out, the rent was $50 a week higher because the house was more appealing.

I never used the equity in Ingleburn; I didn't really need to. I was growing my portfolio, so the next time I bought property, I was using equity from Rockdale. The thing to remember is that when you use your equity in a property, it does increase your loan amount, so continuously using equity increases your debt.

I managed to pay off Ingleburn's $220 000 mortgage in about three years by using equity and profits from other investment properties. Two years later I sold it for about $409 000. Ingleburn had a lot of capital growth and one of the lowest vacancy rates in the country, so it made a good return for me.

My team and I have helped clients find hundreds of properties to renovate, and I have done more facelifts with my own, but I'm not a renovation company. What I do is help people find properties that are suitable for renovation, then offer advice on *what* and *how* they should renovate to add maximum value to that property. So where do we start?

FINANCING FOR RENOVATION

LLOYD'S STRATEGY

For every $1 you spend on a renovation, you should aim to increase the property value by $3.

 **FEASIBILITY**

When flipping a property, I'm always concerned about capital gains tax and the returns I will make, so I need to do a detailed feasibility study. My rule of thumb is to make sure that once you have completed a good renovation, you'll see a significant difference in value between the property's *before* and *after* valuations, ideally realising a three-dollar increase in value for every dollar spent.

To achieve this result, it is important that you set a budget for the renovation work and stay within that budget. Make a list of what needs to be fixed, and prioritise your spending.

 BIG-PICTURE BUDGET

On top of the renovation itself, there are other costs involved in a renovation project, including the initial property purchase price and stamp duty.

After the renovation, if you're selling, you're paying capital gains tax (CGT) plus the agent's commission on the sale. You might decide to hold it for 12 months and then sell it, to get the 50 per cent reduction in CGT. If you live in the property for at least two of the five years before you sell it, you won't need to pay CGT at all, as it was your primary place of residence. Be sure to get advice from your accountant that's appropriate to your own goals. Weigh up these factors and do the numbers so you can set a firm budget.

Often people think, oh, I just want to renovate a property and flip it. But you need to take care of that big-picture budget *before* you get into the project so you understand what you're doing. Otherwise, you could be hit with a massive tax bill at the end of it all. This is also why I suggest keeping a buffer for unforeseen costs!

🏠 PROFIT ESTIMATE

When you're looking at flipping a property, you must have a reasonable expectation of your likely profit. If you're doing a renovation that's going to take you, for example, six weeks, and you know you're going to flip the property after three months of ownership, then your return will be quite different from what you'd expect if you were doing a structural renovation or developing a property from scratch and selling it 18 months later.

You can't expect to make $500000 of profit in six weeks. You need to be realistic and make sure you run the numbers properly. Again, I recommend having a really good team to advise you so your head remains clear, because you can't do everything yourself.

The more you educate yourself about what you're getting yourself into, the better off you're going to be, because you'll have a realistic goal, a realistic turnaround and a realistic profit in mind. You'll be clear on what may be achievable.

🏠 A RENO-READY PROPERTY

Finding the right property to renovate involves not only finding a candidate that fits your strategy; it also has to require a manageable amount of work and tick all the boxes for where it's located as well, so you get that three-for-one financial return on your budget.

🏠 LOCATIONS WITH COMPARABLE SALES

The key to ensuring a profit is to look at comparable sales in the area before choosing a property for renovation. For example, if you're looking at buying a four-bedroom house in a particular area for, say, $500 000 and updating it, you need to look at what renovated four-bedroom houses are selling for in that area. If that's only around $520 000, it's not the right suburb for you, because you're not going to make any money by upgrading it once you factor in the costs.

You need to find locations where you can buy a property for $500 000, say, and do a renovation for $30 000, then have it valued at around $600 000. That way it actually has that three-for-one value you want.

STRUCTURAL RENOVATIONS

Structural renovations can be a bit of a minefield and will often require council approvals. They're not something I necessarily advocate, especially if you're on a smallish budget.

For a structural renovation, such as adding an extra room, you really need to look at how much it's going to improve the property. You might be able to knock down a wall — as long as it's not load-bearing — to open up a living room. Or you might be able to turn a three-bedroom house into a four-bedroom house by *adding* a wall.

You might be able to add an extension to the house, though this will usually require council approvals too. The sort of property that would benefit from a structural renovation is likely to be pretty rundown, so you'll almost certainly need a licensed builder or qualified tradie to do the work, which will cost you more money.

The less you spend, the greater your chance of actually making money from the project.

USING ARCHITECTS

For a bigger job that requires an architect, such as an extension, the architect should be quite separate from the builder. If they work for the same company, that company will charge you an overhead on top of the architect's fee so they can pay all their tradies and still make a profit.

Approach an architect for the design, then take their plans to the tradie or the company that's going to build the extension. Shop around and get two or three quotes independent of any builder's connections.

COSMETIC RENOVATIONS

Rather than major changes requiring structural work, I recommend making cosmetic renovations to update your investments. This usually means looking for properties that need an upgrade of the kitchen and bathrooms, because that's what adds the most value to residential properties. The basic cosmetic updates I look at are landscaping, painting, flooring, kitchen and bathroom upgrades, window coverings and doors.

'UNIQUE' PROPERTIES

If you can see past ugly wallpaper and dated vanities and light fittings, or imagine how a new kitchen could open up the living space in an older home, you may find yourself in an advantageous position with less competition and more room for negotiation on the property. Houses that lack storage, air-conditioning, attractive features or gardens are frequently dismissed by buyers before they even view the property. But these can be simple, inexpensive fixes, and if you're buying the property as an investment, they will be tax deductible and increase the eventual rental income.

OUTDOORS

Often prospective tenants and buyers will do a 'drive-by' of a property to see whether it's actually worth going to the busy weekend inspection. This is why it's worth doing some landscaping. In new estates, councils often recommend adding native plants that are local to the area.

If the property looks rundown from the street, consider painting the exterior and putting in a new front door. A security door can add value for safety-conscious potential buyers. Mend and paint the front fence and make sure your letterbox is in good condition and clearly labelled.

PAINTING

A fresh coat of paint inside and out will instantly give your property a fresh feel as well as increasing its street appeal. Keep the colours neutral — whites, creams and greys — as these will provide a blank canvas for the buyer who's thinking of making this place their home. If the exterior of the house is brick, you could render and paint it for a sleek, modern look.

FLOORING

If the property needs new floor coverings, you can add instant value there. Replace an old carpet or rip it all out. If you're lucky you'll find floorboards underneath that just need some sanding and varnish. Or you can put down floating bamboo or hardwood floors.

DOORS

It's important to have a decent door at the front. Go for big solid one, for security reasons, and you might choose something with a decorative feature such as a stained-glass window.

LIGHTING

Depending on how rundown the house is, you might look at upgrading the light fittings, adding functional varieties such as downlights, and new light switches, including dimmers.

WINDOWS

Consider replacing the window coverings. If the property has dated curtains, look at replacing them with roller blinds or venetian blinds — whichever best suits the property.

CLIMATE

Heating, solar panels and air-conditioning are demanded by the market in certain locations. If you buy a house in Brisbane or Cairns, for example, you should always put air-con in if it isn't already installed. In Hobart and even Melbourne, where the winters can be cold, a reverse-cycle air conditioner with a good heating mode is a big plus.

RENOVATING THE KITCHEN

When it comes to adding the most value to a property, you can't go past kitchen and bathroom renovations. They are also the most expensive, though, so you need to be strategic. Upgrading doesn't mean you go and whack in a brand-new kitchen or bathroom without first doing your homework.

If you are buying a property with the strategy of renovating it to add value, look for a kitchen that can be updated. There are plenty of improvements you can make without replacing the whole kitchen, if doing so isn't within your budget.

You can improve a kitchen by painting the walls and even painting the cupboards and drawers, and updating the handles. You can even replace drawers without replacing the whole kitchen; self-closing drawers are a popular modern feature.

If you've got really old wooden or laminate benchtops, you could swap them with timeless stone benchtops. That is an instantly impressive feature in any kitchen. Consider putting some nice pendant lighting above the benchtop. A stylish splashback is always appealing, too.

If replacing everything, be careful not to overcapitalise with a massively expensive kitchen. You can buy a flat pack fit-out for around $6000 and if you can install it yourself, that will save a lot of money. If you get a professional to install it, it costs a bit more but will ensure quality work.

🏠 RENOVATING THE BATHROOM

The strategy for bathroom renovation is similar. Simply upgrading fittings and painting can save you a lot. Don't put in new things for the sake of it, as you might if it were your own home. With an investment, you need to look at how much any renovation is going to add to the property's value, so it's important to focus on form and function.

You might be able to update the existing shower with frameless shower doors or put in a new vanity. Replace any cracked tiles. When Renee and I were renovating the Lewisham property, we replaced the tiles and did some waterproofing of the shower because there were a couple of leaks. We didn't have to replace the whole bathroom to make it a whole lot better.

🏠 RENOVATING STRATA PROPERTIES

Buying a strata property in a densely populated suburb like Manly or Fitzroy is not a sensible choice if you're looking to renovate, as there are likely to be restrictions on what you're allowed to do in these suburbs. Often you'll need to get permission from the body corporate if you want to put in air-con or for any noisy internal work that might disturb your neighbours. A house in the suburbs is less likely to throw up such obstacles.

CHARACTER HOMES: WEATHERBOARD OR BRICK?

It's a personal choice. I do have some weatherboard homes in my portfolio, but these days I prefer brick homes as they make good, solid investment properties. You can also render brick homes. On the other hand, weatherboard homes can have more character, and you can paint them to add to their appeal.

LEWISHAM: MY FIRST CHARACTER HOME RENOVATION

The second property I renovated was Lewisham, the first house Renee and I bought together. The house was 100 years old and had already been renovated when we bought it for $785 000. So inside it looked brand-new, and the exterior had also been painted and looked great.

However, some of the renovations turned out to be a bit 'dodgy'. While we were living there, the bi-fold French doors at the back wouldn't close properly, and we had to put a chair against the door. When it rained, water would come in under the doors and flood the house. Water also came through the downlights when it rained because of a hole in the roof. Then the bathroom tiles started to fall off the walls and the shower door wouldn't close properly. Then some of the kitchen appliances broke down ... then the heating ceased to work. And then, the final insult, we couldn't close the front door properly!

We'd been living there for about seven years when we started looking for our dream house. When it came time to sell Lewisham, we knew we'd need to maximise our return. We ended up doing a full renovation of the bathroom and got new bi-fold doors for the back because by now the wood was rotting. The new doors were actually made of metal and really nice glass. I did the patio out the back and some painting.

Renee had a lot of input into the design. I guess it's just one of those things; she chooses what she wants and I pay for it! We didn't agree on the colour of the new tiles for the bathroom, so we got hundreds of tile samples and went looking in the showrooms. It was fun, but if we were ever to get on *The Block*, I'm sure we'd do each other's head in! When I gave Renee the lead role in this type of renovation, though, it always worked out well. In fact, as I write this, we're planning the renovation of a couple of our bathrooms here at Lilli Pilli, and we're in the middle of another conversation about ... tile selection!

We made Lewisham look really nice just as we were selling, and then we thought, we may as well stay here now — we should have renovated years ago! We ended up selling in early 2018 for $1.3 million.

That renovation certainly helped get us a good price under what could have been difficult circumstances. The market was starting to slow down at the time. Also, the property was in a good suburb but not a good street, and it was on a busy road. We were happy to live there, but I would never buy it as an investment property. The location made it difficult to sell.

HERITAGE-LISTED PROPERTIES

Some older, character homes may have heritage restrictions. If you want to renovate a heritage-listed property, you'll need to check with council about what alterations are and are not permitted. You may need to keep the original balustrades, for example, or keep the fence to a certain height or a specific style. You may not be able to add an extension or change the period façade. The control plans, like the local environmental plan, are specific to every area, so it's not 'one size fits all'.

MANAGING YOUR OWN RENOVATION

How much management should you take on yourself? If you get someone else to manage a group of tradies, you're essentially hiring a renovation company, and that's going to cost you a lot more, which will reduce your profit. I don't recommend that path when you're starting out. You need to be proactive and communicate directly with the tradies.

WHERE TO START

You need to get the more complicated jobs out of the way first. Start with the major work. Plumbing might be the first major task, but if you need an electrician, get them to come and have a look first.

If you're putting in a new kitchen, do that next. If you engage a kitchen company to replace your kitchen it will cost around $20 000 to $30 000, and that's your whole renovation budget gone.

Instead, go to Bunnings or Ikea and buy a kitchen there, which will be much cheaper and will be something you can probably install for yourself. If you're not handy or you don't have the time to do it, hiring a handyman who will charge you an hourly rate of around $40 will be much more cost-effective.

WHERE TO FIND GOOD TRADIES

Online is probably not the way to go. First-hand recommendations from family and friends are usually the best place to start. If asked, I can recommend tradies I know and have worked with.

If I recommend a painter, the painter doesn't work for me and I'm not getting any kind of a commission for recommending them. I also don't get any commission from brokers, accountants or solicitors, and I tell my clients that upfront. I recommend professionals only if I believe they'll do a good job for my client.

Word of mouth can work well. For example, a carpenter you've used, whose work you're happy with, might be able to recommend an electrician or tiler. You can build up your own network by just getting the right people on board and then asking them for recommendations. They become an extension of your dream team, and you can use them for further renovation work in the same area later.

ASSESSING QUOTES

I recommend getting quotes from three different professionals for every service you need. Three should give you a good measure of cost, and a choice of value so you can be confident you're getting good-quality work.

HIGH QUOTES

If all the quotes are similar, it means they're probably all pretty legit. If one quote is really high, then it may be because of hidden fees that are not generally disclosed. Or perhaps they have quoted for items or services you don't require.

IF THE QUOTE SEEMS TOO LOW...

I'm a firm believer that if anything sounds too good to be true, it probably is.

If everyone else is charging $2000 for a job and one guy is offering to do it for $200, you need to ask why. Are they just trying to undercut their competition? Or are they going to spend an hour on a job the other quoters would take two days to complete? That cheaper tradie might not give you a particularly good result.

Sometimes they might offer a legit explanation like, 'Well, I have low overheads. I work for myself and only have to pay myself'. Companies have overheads because they're running their business out of a premises and paying employees, which will affect their pricing. You do need to ask questions to find out.

HELPING TO CUT BACK THOSE COSTS

It is definitely worth keeping the lines of communication with the tradies open, and asking what you can do to reduce that bottom-line quote. Offer to do some of the time-consuming 'odd jobs' so they can just come in, do their thing and leave. You don't want to pay a builder $60 an hour to cart rubbish out to the bin. Of course, you've got to do those odd jobs safely, which may mean wearing a hard hat, boots, safety glasses and gloves.

Ask your tradies or your builder:

- What can I do to help prepare for your job?
- How can I help keep the site clean?
- What can I do to help the build come in on time?

GETTING THE BUILD FINISHED ON TIME

A lot of builds go over time, but if there is anything you can do to keep things on schedule, this proactivity can help keep such overruns in check.

Stay on top of the things that require the longest delivery lead times, such as joinery and windows. Make sure you answer all the necessary questions. Be sure you've signed off on your window colours, cabinetry colour and benchtops, and got those jobs into production. That's where you'll save money.

Tradies are notorious for not showing up on time and forgetting to come back. When you're managing a renovation you need to monitor and control that in order to come in on budget and on schedule.

You need to be comfortable with the contract you're signing *before* the work begins. Has the builder or tradie given you a fixed time for when the work will be completed? Will it be done in six weeks or eight weeks? Try to lock them down.

Painting may take only two days. If you're hiring a painter, you might say, 'This is a rental property. It's my business. I need this job done by the end of next week. Can you do it or not?'

When booking tradies, you might say, 'We want you to come on this date and it needs to be finished by this date. Can you do it?' It's either yes or no. Then have a contract signed to ensure that happens, including a late completion clause stating that if it isn't completed on time, the builder will need to pay you liquidated damages. This clause is usually standard in HIA (Housing Industry Assocation) contracts, but make sure there is a decent dollar amount next to it.

OUTSOURCING YOUR RENOVATION

If you can't liaise with each tradie because the property is far from where you live, a property manager will help with giving tradies access.

As your portfolio grows and your own time has more demands on it, outsourcing more jobs tips over into being the most economical option. For example, I renovated a property in Toowoomba in 2015. When I'd bought the property in 2013, my strategy was to buy and hold for long-term growth, but now it needed renovation, so I updated the kitchen, put in new floor coverings, did some painting and fixed a few minor things.

This was the first time I had outsourced jobs to tradies. It cost only about $8000, with the tradies giving me mate's rates as they had done other jobs for me, and had even been involved in some of my duplex builds. Afterwards, I managed to increase the rent by about $40 a week. It's still in my investment portfolio.

As another example, at the same time we were renovating Lewisham, I was also renovating Wallsend, and I used a trusted real estate agent to manage the project.

MY WALLSEND RENOVATION

Wallsend is a suburb of Newcastle. I bought the property in 2014 for $388 000, but I didn't renovate until 2018. It was another character home on a large block, a really cute property. I always had an exit strategy for this property, because it was also going to help us buy our dream home.

Renee loved it. She thought, I'm going to buy this one and renovate it. She had all these nice ideas, but then she got busy and decided not to take it on. Wallsend is not easy to reach when you live in Sydney, so I leased it out. It was positively geared, a particularly good rental property in a very good suburb, and it did well. But when it came time to sell, I found that the tenants hadn't looked after the place as well as I would have liked, so there was damage that had to be repaired. We held back a little of the bond, which covered the basics.

I outsourced the Wallsend upgrade because I was not on location. I got quotes and hired chippies, carpet people and painters. We updated the kitchen and the floor coverings and got a full paint job. There was a lot of work done there.

The person I had managing that renovation was actually the real estate agent I had contracted to sell the property. He'd managed a couple of my other properties over the years, and I'd bought properties through him for my buyer's agency clients. So we had a good working relationship. He could help organise quotes because he had contacts in the local area. He would let the tradies in and oversee the work as well.

I lined everything up and gave us a maximum of 21 days, but we had it done within 14 days, and then it was on the market. The Newcastle market was on a downturn, so we were lucky. I turned down a few offers but I sold it within four weeks, for just under $600 000.

MY ROCKDALE RENOVATION

I renovated Rockdale in 2021. I had never done much to it, but after 18 years it was starting to look very tired. I ended up painting the whole place, putting in new carpets, doing some work in the kitchen, getting a new air-conditioning system and new blinds, and upgrading the bathroom. Now it looks like new. I may sell it at some stage, because apartments do tend to get a bit rundown eventually. For now I'm keeping it for cashflow.

I outsourced that one. Again, I got quotes — three from painters and three from air-conditioning suppliers — to make sure I got the best deal. The reno was done in three weeks, but work wasn't going on every day. The property was vacant at the time.

CASE STUDY
MANUFACTURING $61 000 THROUGH RENOVATION

Liam, an ambitious young man in his early thirties, came to me after reading my first book, *Positively Geared*. He had the deposit and wanted to buy his first investment property and build a strategy with me for future investments and developments.

(continued)

THE BRIEF

As a low-income earner with a very limited borrowing capacity, Liam was in the market for a $260 000 property, and he wanted to buy in Sydney!

I explained that he couldn't afford a home in Sydney just yet, and advised that he start building a portfolio so later he'd be able to buy where he wanted to and achieve other life goals.

Liam was young, with no dependants. He had loads of energy and drive and spare time up his sleeve, so an older property with potential for minor renovations was a great fit for him.

We decided that regional NSW would be the best area, with potential for growth and instant equity from a cosmetic renovation. After due diligence, we chose a town close to a university, hospitals and multiple private schools, with a great cafe culture — perfect for a rental.

THE ACQUISITION

We needed to find Liam the right home — one with good bones that would benefit from an upgrade and achieve a good rental yield.

After shortlisting a number of properties in a competitive market, we found a large, flat block of more than 1000 sqm with a classic 1960s three-bed, one-bath weatherboard home on it.

It was a perfect opportunity for Liam to get started. By performing cosmetic renovations at a small cost he could gain instant equity. The large block also showed potential for further development down the track.

The property was listed at $258 000 and we were able to negotiate a price of $229 000. The saving of $29 000 well and truly paid for the stamp duty and renovations.

We knew there was good potential to increase the value of the home, as comparable homes in that area had a median sales price of $337 000.

THE RENOVATION

Liam completed most of the renovations himself, with some help from friends and family, which helped keep costs down. Most of the work involved updating the kitchen, including removing a non-load-bearing wall to increase its size and give it a more modern, open-plan feel.

Liam was lucky enough to have a neighbour who was a plasterer, so he was able to get help from someone he trusted at a good rate.

He bought most of the supplies from Bunnings, including a Kaboodle kitchen, which he found easy to install himself. He removed the bulky overhead cupboards to make the kitchen feel larger and added a full-length pantry for practical use.

He found beautiful hardwood floors under the kitchen linoleum. He sanded and varnished these, which added to the aesthetics of the property while maintaining some of its original charm. Liam also gutted and fully renovated the bathroom, including beautiful floor-to-ceiling tiles and a stunning deep freestanding bath.

To add further charm to the property, Liam painted it throughout and added new window furnishings.

THE RESULT

After the work was completed, a valuation of the property was set at $290 000.

(continued)

Liam had spent just under $20 000 on renovations and added $61 000 to the property's value. This meant that for every dollar he'd spent, Liam got a return of just over three dollars.

Before the renovations, the property was rented for $310 a week. Liam was able to rent it out immediately after the renovations for $360, a $50 a week increase and an 8.1 per cent gross rental yield.

This strategy allowed Liam to draw on the equity in this property to purchase his next investment property.

THE NUMBERS

Budget:	$260 000
Property price:	listed at $258 000, purchased for $229 000, saving $29 000
Renovation:	$20 000
Valuation post-renovation:	$290 000
Increase in value:	$61 000
Rental before renovation:	$310 a week
Rental after renovation:	$360 a week

CHAPTER 9
READ THE MARKETS

Read the Australian property markets like a pro

 Reading the markets can be challenging and confusing, and will often lead to analysis paralysis in less experienced investors. They don't know where they are in a particular market cycle. They're unclear on what to look for and will wait six months to 'time the market'. The remedy is to conduct thorough research—then act. In this chapter I'll provide a general overview of how the Australian property markets work and what to look for.

There's a quote I like to share: 'No-one's ever made money by waiting'.

So many people wait to buy. They think, If I wait a bit longer, I may get a better deal. If I wait, the market may crash and then I'll get a better price. But nobody who has actually become wealthy through property investment has got there through the strategy of waiting.

I can't make this point too often. People ask me all the time, 'When's the best time to buy?'

My advice is simple: *now is always the right time to buy*. You need to get moving, not sit on the sidelines and wait to see if the market crashes so you can get a better deal, because that almost never happens.

If you're ready to buy, if you've got your finance in place, do it now, because there are always good opportunities, even in a hot market.

Don't think, *Oh, I can't buy anywhere at the moment*. No matter how bullish the markets are, there are still winning strategies on how to buy in these conditions. There are *always* ways to buy well.

If you're buying a primary residence, there are ways to make that work too, because if you wait, in 12 months' time you might just end up being in another cycle where things are booming again. With the benefit of hindsight you'll recognise that in the time you sat on the sidelines, property prices continued to increase.

Mentally, you need to be in a position to say, 'Yep, I've done my research. I'm confident in this market and I know I can move on this next good deal'.

THE PROPERTY CLOCK

When making sense of market cycles, I like to use the analogy of a clock. The top of the clock — 12 o'clock — is the top of the cycle. Six o'clock is the bottom of the cycle. The period between six o'clock and 12 o'clock is the growth phase of the cycle, and from twelve o'clock down to six marks the decline of the cycle.

⏱ AUSTRALIAN PROPERTY-MARKET CYCLE FACTS

Here are a few factors to keep in mind when thinking about property cycles:

1. The property clock isn't a constant exact science. For example, during the pandemic boom, the property clock went out the window as almost every market saw huge growth.

2. There is no universal property cycle; rather, there are many property markets across the country. So I always refer to Australian property markets in the plural. Equally, there are many Australian market cycles.

3. Not every area in Australia experiences great cycles. Markets that see great growth, such as Sydney and Melbourne, have real cycles in which generally, over a seven to 10-year period, you can see huge growth. Eventually the cycle will likely slow down and prices will plateau or decline slightly before the next growth phase begins. Other markets, such as many regional areas or a capital city like Adelaide, are a bit softer and see much slower growth.

4. Different markets move at a different pace — and, more importantly, at different times. You might buy in Sydney during a growth phase, but once Sydney gets to the peak of its cycle it's no longer the right time to buy there. So if you're thinking of buying an investment property during that period, consider buying in another area where the market is starting to rise, which could be Brisbane, as historically that city follows Sydney's lead.

5. One other thing to consider is that regional areas — those country towns — don't really have cycles in the same way that cities do.

⏱ TIMING THE MARKET TO MITIGATE RISK

Being able to predict which markets are likely to boom really comes down to doing your due diligence: researching things like infrastructure development, government spending, population growth and jobs growth, and focusing on economies that are more susceptible to large-cycle growth.

When you do this, 'timing the market' is not so critical, because what you buy depends more on strategy and on what you're trying to achieve.

At the same time, you can also do your research on which cities can fluctuate too much, such as Perth, which is too reliant on the resources sector, or the Gold Coast, which has had many ebbs and flows over the years because of its over-reliance on the tourism sector. In these markets, a boom is usually followed by a decline in prices.

Wherever you buy, I don't recommend doing so at the peak of a cycle or at its downturn. Some commentators say you should buy in a booming market, but I disagree. Ideally, you should buy *before* the market booms.

LLOYD'S STRATEGY

Buy before the boom.

Whatever market you're in, you should be buying at the start of the growth cycle, at around seven or eight o'clock on the property clock.

HOW DO YOU KNOW A MARKET IS REALLY STARTING TO MOVE OR TURN?

You can't know exactly when a market is going to peak, just as you can't tell when a market has hit the bottom of its cycle. To spot the start of a boom, you need to keep an eye on the following developments:

1. There's a decrease in 'days on the market' — that is, how long a property has been advertised before it sells.

2. You'll see an increase in attendance numbers at open homes.

3. Auction clearance rates start to rise — that is, more properties are selling under the hammer.

As explained, the cycles move at different times, and there are plenty of fantastic regional and coastal locations to buy in, where capital growth is steady. These markets also tend to have better rental yields, which spells better cashflow.

Another way to mitigate your risk is to find properties you can do a bit to improve, as discussed in the previous chapters on creating your own equity. If you add some value to your property, you won't need to rely as much on what the cycle is doing, particularly if you're buying in regional centres.

SENTIMENT, SUPPLY AND DEMAND

Identifying and reacting to market sentiment is a part of understanding the markets. It's important to really educate yourself on this, because some price increases are quite artificial. It's amazing, for example, how much sentiment changes depending on the elected government and especially their policies on negative gearing, which can either entice or repel investors.

When the Reserve Bank decreased interest rates in 2020, trying to stimulate inflation, that kept house prices moving along and heated the markets up. When the property markets heat up, FOMO kicks in, as people start to worry about missing out and that there isn't much stock left on the market. And this artificially raises prices.

The problem is exacerbated by the reluctance of vendors to list their properties, because with prices starting to increase they think they'll get more by selling 'next year'. You need to monitor this carefully, because listings can increase at the drop of a hat if either market sentiment or people's situations change.

That's where it's really important to have a strategy, so you know how a particular property purchase will fit into your portfolio.

I like to invest in areas with a fairly low supply of properties coupled with high demand, because that's what's really going to push your property value up. It's harder to buy a property in areas where there's high demand and not much supply and you may end up paying more than you want to, because at the end of the day you're paying what the market determines. This is where good negotiation skills and good connections with local real estate agents are important.

So while you could worry about overpaying, you're simply paying market value on the day. And if you buy into a really good area that has all the amenities and good infrastructure, then that should be a good long-term investment.

Conversely, you definitely *don't* want to get into a market that's *oversupplied*, which is what we found with units in the Melbourne CBD, or townhouses and units in Brisbane from around 2015 on. There are certain pockets in Sydney as well, in the apartment market, that are oversupplied, with too many of them for sale at the same time. This puts downward pressure on both sales prices and rental demand, so you need to be careful of all that.

BOOM-BUST MARKETS

People often think that when a market has been down for a while, property in that market will be a good investment because surely it will soon be on the way up. That's not true of all markets, all the time, though.

From 2010 to 2020 two capital city markets in Australia — Perth and Darwin — experienced an overall decrease in property prices. That was because both are too reliant on the resources sector. This is particularly true of Perth. You might decide that Perth is a good place to park money now, because the prices are down and they're surely going to start increasing again. But being one of the only markets in Australia to experience a decline in prices — as was the case when the resources sector declined after the mining boom ended around 2012–13 — is not a good place to be. Perth has been getting a lot of growth in recent years, mainly because it had a low starting point after four or five years of negative growth. That in itself is a problem.

It's also a good idea to stay right away from one-horse mining towns that rely on only one sector because sooner or later that industry will experience large declines. You may be seeing lots of growth and enjoying a really high rental yield — then a mine closes or something changes in the industry that town depends on, and you lose it all. I experienced that in one of my properties in central Queensland, so I know first-hand what can happen.

This is why investing in places that have a lot of industries and economic drivers is really important. I'll go further into this when we talk about due diligence in chapter 10.

Now consider the Gold Coast. You may have thought about investing in property on the Gold Coast, knowing you can get good properties there for under market value. But you need to be careful of investing somewhere where the market keeps fluctuating. Driven by tourism, the

Gold Coast was hit hard during the COVID-19 pandemic when the tourism industry was shut down. Hosting the Olympics — coming to Queensland in 2032 — is sure to help many of these Queensland markets that rely on tourism, though. I expect it will see a lot of growth and once again become a good area to invest in.

$1 MILLION TO INVEST

I want to give you an example of looking at the different markets from the perspective of someone with a $1 million budget, and of the different strategies you can apply when you have a certain budget. Should you spend your whole budget on one property? Or are you better off breaking it down? People in this position sometimes come to me for advice, like my client Mary who ended up rentvesting. I tell them, with that much to spend, you've got a couple of options.

If you want to live in Sydney, for example, you're not going to get much of a home to live in, and you're not going to be able to find much of an investment in Sydney for that amount, either. But in another state or region, you could find a really good property for a million dollars.

If you were to buy a $1 million investment property in Sydney, you would probably get only about $650 a week in rent. So you'd be heavily negatively geared — and that, depending on your income, could well prevent you from moving forward to another property.

For example, if you borrow 90 per cent of a $1 million property and put down a $90 000 deposit plus stamp duty, you've essentially got a loan there of more than $900 000. And if you're getting only $650 a week in rent, that will come nowhere near to covering the mortgage payments, which might be closer to $900 per week, depending on your interest rate. Then you've also got your rates, all your outgoings on the property, and potential repairs and maintenance. If it's a unit, you'll probably have strata costs as well. And because it's heavily negatively geared and you have maxed out your $1 million borrowing capacity, you're probably going to get stuck, and you won't be able to move forward to another property.

NEGATIVE GEARING AS A STRATEGY

I recommend aiming for positively geared properties, but negative gearing can definitely work for some property investors.

Whether you opt for negatively or positively geared properties really depends on your property investment strategy and what you're trying to achieve. Some people on high incomes might choose to negatively gear a property for tax reasons. That's not a property strategy; it's an outcome. Perhaps it can win you a good tax refund, but you really need to look at your long-term goals.

You also need to look at where you are in terms of your own finances and income, because sometimes you'll need a positive-cashflow property, or at least one that's neutrally geared, for the banks to lend you money to buy your next property. We look at instant equity, cashflow and capital growth because we're focusing on your long-term goals, and how you're going to get there.

We also need to think about your exit strategy. You might want to have some negatively geared properties in your portfolio — I've got some — simply because they're strategically located. They might be properties you want to hold for the long term, and they will be high growth properties.

A property I bought for my sons in 2020 is positively geared, but only because I put down quite a big deposit on it. Strictly, it's a negatively geared property because of its location: a blue-chip suburb of Sydney. When I buy such properties, I always balance them by doing dual-income properties such as duplexes, located in areas that will get me a really good cashflow too.

A property's cashflow is very important. Cashflow is always good, as *it enables you to continue to invest*.

INVESTING FURTHER FROM HOME

With $1 million, you could buy two properties in areas other than Sydney.

For example, you could buy a property in Brisbane and one in Adelaide, and spend about $500 000 on each. Those properties will also produce much better cashflow. Depending on the suburb, the rent on a $500 000 Brisbane property is probably going to be around $460 to $480 a week. Assuming you paid a 10 per cent deposit on the property, your loan would be only around $450 000. Your weekly mortgage payments would then be around $450 a week. You can already see how the cashflow here is much better than you'd get for a Sydney rental property, and will serve your portfolio well.

The banks see that rent coming in from your first property as income. When you get your loan revised for your second property, that extra income will probably increase your serviceability, which means you'll be able to borrow more, so it has put you in a much better situation. Most banks will accept only around 70 per cent of a property's rental income towards serviceability, up to a maximum yield of 6 per cent. You can see why we need to increase cashflow on investment properties so we don't get stuck.

If you bought your first property in Brisbane and you're getting $480 a week in rent, then you decide to buy another property, the bank might say, 'Yeah, you can still borrow another $600 000'.

So you were originally planning on borrowing $1 million; now you're looking at borrowing more than $1 million, because you've got a good rent coming in from your first property. Then you might go and buy a property in Adelaide and spend only $400 000 on it, which still leaves you with $200 000 in borrowing capacity.

Your $400 000 Adelaide property will probably bring in about $400 to $420 a week in rent, to give you a yield of 5.2 to 5.4 per cent. You can still get a loan to purchase *another* property. In a town in regional Victoria like Wodonga, for example, you might be able to buy house for only $300 000.

Rather than buying that one negatively geared property in Sydney, you've now bought three properties, all with good cashflow. What's more, two of them are in capital cities, so you've made a really good start to your portfolio. I told you about my client Mary who successfully used this strategy to build a nest egg plus income while rentvesting in Sydney.

I always share this strategy with clients, because it can set them up. It's the difference between having one property and being maxed out, and having three properties and being in a position where the banks will happily still lend to you.

Of course, part of the strategy is not to cross-securitise and to go to different banks for your different mortgages.

STRATEGIES FOR INVESTING MORE THAN $1 MILLION

Sometimes you may be able to borrow more. For example, at the time of writing I have just started working with a client who can borrow about $3 million, and we're developing an investment strategy.

How much you would need to put down to borrow $3 million depends on several factors. If you're going to borrow at 90 per cent on all your properties, you'll have to pay Lenders Mortgage Insurance and stamp duty, and you'll need at least $300 000 in the bank. All up, then, you'll need at least $550 000 or $600 000 cash available.

If you can borrow $3 million, though, obviously you have a higher income or are a bit further down the track with building your portfolio, and your strategy and goals may be a little bit different. This particular client is happy to have some negative-cashflow properties because he has an income that can sustain it, and he wants to buy in the highest growth areas. This is where I need to listen especially closely to what the client wants.

In this case, he wants to buy a $2 million investment property in Sydney, even if it brings him only $1200 a week in rent (a 3.12 per cent yield), because it's going to give him good growth. He's happy to sustain some negative cashflow because over the long term that property's going to increase in value. His accountant has also advised him to use property to effectively reduce his taxable income. This means he will need to pay the difference between the rent he receives and his mortgage repayments from his own income. This will be around $600 a week on this property, so it's negatively geared by $600 a week! You can see why I don't like negative gearing. But if your income can sustain it and you need that tax break because of your high income, speak to your accountant.

For this client's $3 million, we'll be looking at buying three properties in three different cities. One will be an expensive negatively geared property in Sydney, one will be in Brisbane and one will be in Melbourne. The Sydney property won't necessarily cost $2 million; it could be $1.6 or $1.8 million and achieve the same result. This will also afford him a bit more borrowing power to move forward with the second and third purchases.

The one in Brisbane will be cashflow-neutral, the one in Melbourne will be slightly negatively geared and the one in Sydney will be negatively geared, because part of his strategy is to offset some of his income on tax. To my mind, you should never buy property just because you want to save on tax, but it is an outcome that you need to factor into your strategy.

WITH MORE CAPITAL, SHOULD YOUR STRATEGY BE FOR HIGH GROWTH OR CASHFLOW?

Of course that depends on your circumstances. The client in this example initially wanted two negatively geared properties in his $3 million portfolio. We'll buy three, because that's how we ended up formulating his strategy. But that's not a prescription for everyone with $3 million. Someone else might want nothing negatively geared in their portfolio.

This is where it comes down to the investor's personal goals. Someone else might buy six properties in different areas in order to build up a lot of positive cashflow. Another might do just one townhouse development or a couple of duplexes. There's a heap of things you can do when you've got more money.

One of my clients is spending about $3.6 million on a townhouse development on the NSW Central Coast. He spent a couple of million dollars on the land and now he's going to spend about $1.6 million building on it. Ultimately he plans to sell those four townhouses at a big profit.

Someone else might just buy and hold a lot of assets in capital cities. With $5 million you could probably buy 10 properties in Adelaide at $500 000 each. Yet another investor could buy five million-dollar properties in Sydney, though that is getting harder these days.

As you can see, it comes down to what you're trying to achieve. In the end, most people have the same goal in mind: gaining financial freedom and being able to look after their family. If you've got kids, you want to be able to provide for them, to create a legacy for them. Most of us have that much in common, but we'll often choose different paths to get to that goal using property.

WHERE DO HIGH-VOLUME INVESTORS LOOK?

A client of mine in Melbourne has 35 properties. I haven't helped him buy every one of those properties, but he uses me when he wants to purchase in New South Wales, Queensland and, sometimes, depending on his strategy, in Victoria too. He owns properties in other states too, though he has purchased those without my help. It seems like he owns property just about everywhere, so he's a high-net-worth client, but he started out with little, built up his own business and has worked hard to build up his portfolio and become financially free.

He has always had a strategy in place to make sure he buys the best-value property. He uses my services as a buyer's agent to help him get the right property in the right location at the right price.

It's worth reiterating that these top-end clients are not really my focus. I like to work with anyone, but especially 'mum and dad investors' who are trying to get ahead. A lot of my more successful clients who've built large portfolios had very humble beginnings, often on low incomes, as I did myself — and we strategised from there. I love to inspire others to achieve what I have.

Remember, if I can do it, so can you.

WHY MANUFACTURE GROWTH?

I want you to understand that you shouldn't be just relying on trying to predict market cycle upswings for when you buy, because there are plenty of other ways to make money on property.

If you've invested in Sydney or Melbourne over the past 10 or 20 years, then you've probably made a lot of money. Growth on this scale has not been equalled anywhere else in Australia.

All this growth means things are very different in Sydney and Melbourne now from how they were 20 years ago. For example, my Rockdale apartment, which I bought for $260 000, is worth between $700 000 and $800 000 today. I have leveraged off the increased equity from my Rockdale property on around four occasions to further grow my portfolio.

You can do the same today, regardless of the specific property. For example, if you have $350 000 to spend, you can buy a house for $325 000 and renovate it. With that kind of money, you'd have to buy a positive-cashflow property in a regional location. But while other markets don't experience the same booms as Sydney and Melbourne do, they also don't experience the same declines, so you can still achieve good growth.

What's important is that you can still invest in those other areas, but you'll need to look at other ways to make your money there, such as adding value to your property. This is because while you can generally pick when a market is starting to rise and moving to seven or eight o'clock in the market cycle, that doesn't guarantee prices will *keep* increasing in that particular market. To better control things, you should keep adding value to your investment. If you do a development, a subdivision or a renovation, you're effectively creating your own little growth cycle within your portfolio.

That's something I love to do, and a strategy that has been very kind to me over the years.

WHAT TO LOOK FOR IN A REGIONAL MARKET

The NSW Central Coast is a region where I'm looking at buying another investment property right now. Not only is it a great place in which to invest, but it's an attractive place to live, especially for families and retirees looking for more space and a more relaxing lifestyle. Of course, the fact that so many people are moving there is exactly what makes it such a good investment.

In the following profile I use the Central Coast as an example of what to look for in a market, whether you're hunting for a home or an investment property.

REGIONAL PROFILE: THE NSW CENTRAL COAST – A TOP-PERFORMING MARKET

A BEAUTIFUL LOCATION

The traditional owners of the Central Coast Council area are the Darkinjung, Guringai and Awabakal people. This is an area where beautiful beaches meet pristine national parks and pretty waterways, enjoyed by residents, regular holidaymakers and tourists alike. Attractions include exploring the area's natural treasures through outdoor adventures, encountering native animals at popular wildlife sanctuaries, sampling local food and wine, and enjoying the region's thriving arts scene.

The Central Coast ticks most of the major investment boxes right off the bat:

- **Centrally located.** The region is named for its central location on the coast of New South Wales, 75 kilometres north of the Sydney CBD and about 80 kilometres south of the Newcastle CBD.

- **Highly accessible.** The Central Coast Council area is served by the Sydney–Newcastle Freeway, the Pacific Motorway, the Central Coast Highway, the Pacific Highway, the Sydney–Newcastle railway line and Warnervale Airport.

- **A growing population.** The region is the ninth-largest population centre in Australia and the third-largest in NSW. The Central Coast Council's estimated resident population for 2021 was 354 915, up from 345 809 in 2020, and is forecast to grow to 414 615 by 2036.

  As a region poised for rapid population growth throughout the 2020s, the Central Coast offers enormous development opportunities for those planning new residential, business, educational and visitor facilities.

- **Ripe for development.** At the time of writing the Central Coast Council is well into its 25-year economic development strategy for the Central Coast's northern area.

  Council spent $183 million on infrastructure in 2016–17, and the NSW Government has allocated major funds to upgrading the region's key transport corridors.

  The Council also provides attractive incentives, such as deferred contributions for developers who meet certain conditions, and has one of the fastest development application turnaround times in the state.

- **Great value.** The Central Coast is one of the best-value areas for property in the Greater Sydney basin, with low establishment costs and strong demand. The region's industrial land sits next to major transport infrastructure, logistically halfway between Sydney and Newcastle, and equidistant from Melbourne and Brisbane.

INVESTMENT MARKET BREAKDOWN – A CLOSER LOOK

The council area encompasses 1680 square kilometres, including more than 80 kilometres of coastline. It has discrete natural borders, such as the Hawkesbury River and Lake Macquarie.

More than half of the council area is national parks, nature reserves, beaches and waterways. Rural land is used mainly for farming, timber getting and coal mining for electricity generation.

The population is dispersed across towns, villages and neighbourhoods, including the largest centres of Gosford, Tuggerah-Wyong, Erina, Woy Woy and The Entrance.

LIFESTYLE

The Central Coast region offers an attractive lifestyle for families. It boasts clean beaches, calm coastal lakes and reasonably priced housing. With its moderate climate and accessibility to medical services within the region and in Sydney, the region attracts many retirees. It also has a strong sports participation culture and a growing creative demographic based around musical performance and recording.

TRANSPORT AND INFRASTRUCTURE

The Central Coast links NSW's two largest population centres, Sydney and Newcastle. Some 38 000 people leave the region daily to work, most of them commuting to the Sydney metropolitan area. This makes significant road and rail infrastructure essential. Key links are the F3 freeway and the CityRail network.

VIBRANT CENTRES

The Central Coast has a vibrant retail sector, which is sure to expand with the region's increasing population and business investment. Well-located new housing development will assist in creating settlements that foster a stronger sense of community identity and place.

By 2031, the regional city of Gosford and the Tuggerah–Wyong major centre will be supported by a developing network of town centres, villages and neighbourhoods.

EDUCATION

The Central Coast is well served by education providers, from early childcare through to higher-degree research, with many of the staff trained locally on the Ourimbah campus.

Government and independent primary and secondary schools offer a broad range of choices and a wide variety of additional experiences based on a foundation of academic excellence.

TAFE NSW, community colleges and private registered training organisation (RTO) providers work closely with industry and local businesses. The University of Newcastle — Central Coast campus at Ourimbah attracts students to the region.

LOGISTICS AND WAREHOUSING

The Central Coast's unique location as a link between Sydney, Newcastle and Brisbane is why several logistics companies have chosen the region as a business base.

INVESTMENT MARKET INDUSTRY STRUCTURE

The Central Coast economy comprises a large number of small and medium-sized businesses. At the smaller end, micro- and home-based businesses service the local markets.

The larger employers in the region include the health service, state and local government agencies, several manufacturers, food processors, logistics and distribution centres, construction, clubs, resorts, call centres, large retailers and the education sector. The region has been successful in attracting national and global enterprises.

KEY GROWTH SECTOR: FOOD

The Central Coast is home to a number of familiar food brands found on supermarket shelves around the country. The region has a strong food industry presence and boasts excellent credentials, which makes it an attractive location for food manufacturing and agribusiness. Farmers in the region employ both traditional and advanced methods of intensive agriculture to grow a diverse range of produce.

PROJECTS AND OPPORTUNITIES

Identified by the state government as a key growth area, the NSW Central Coast offers a diverse range of infrastructure investment, property development and capital business opportunities at great value. All these investment opportunities are supported by continuing economic growth, and by the significant public and private investment already occurring in infrastructure, business and residential projects in the region.

The median weekly rental prices have grown steadily in the area (see table 9.1) and the value of building approvals in the Central Coast Council area was $117 million, with 292 residential buildings approved to be built in the 2021–22 FYTD financial year (see figure 9.1).

Houses				Units		
Year (at June)	Central Coast Council area	Greater Sydney	New South Wales	Central Coast Council area	Greater Sydney	New South Wales
2018	$425	$530	$465	$390	$525	$490
2017	$420	$520	$450	$380	$520	$480
2016	$420	$520	$440	$380	$500	$460
2015	$400	$500	$420	$360	$490	$440
2014	$380	$490	$410	$350	$470	$425

Table 9.1: Median weekly rental prices for the NSW Central Coast Council area
Source: Hometrack 2014-2018, Automated Valuation System, presented and compiled by .id (informed decisions)

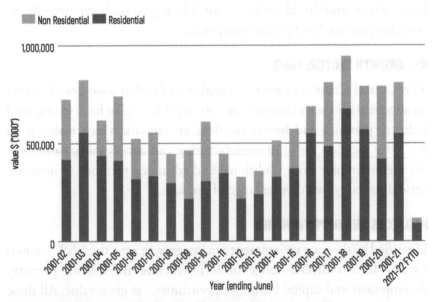

Figure 9.1: Building approvals for the NSW Central Coast Council area
© Commonwealth of Australia
Source: Australian Bureau of Statistics, Building Approvals, Australia, catalogue number 8731.0. Compiled and presented in economy.id by .id (informed decisions)

CHAPTER 10
THE PROPERTY HUNT

Find top locations and properties ripe for investment

 Good research is critically important in the property investment space, whether you're buying a home to live in while watching its value increase over time, or you're building a property portfolio to increase your wealth and work towards your goals. Knowing what to look for will help you nail down a great place to invest, where your money will go further.

WHAT IS DUE DILIGENCE?

We've discussed Australian property markets in general and have looked at the fantastic example of the Central Coast in New South Wales as a top-performing market. Performing due diligence means doing the research needed to identify that kind of market, then making sure it's the right market for you to buy into.

What you're looking for will depend on your strategy. First, though, are you seeking a home or an investment property? One significant difference between the two objectives is that, unlike when buying a home to live in, which will often engage your emotions, you can approach your search and purchase of investment properties entirely pragmatically. When buying to build capital growth and manufacturing equity, you need to be consistently, ruthlessly practical.

Whatever you're looking for, always start with your wish list, which helps establish your goals. It should include your financial and lifestyle goals, such as putting your kids through school, the kind of passive income you want to live off in the future, when you want to semi-retire or retire, or even buying a boat — whatever it is you want in your future.

What's going to help you achieve your first financial goal? Are you going to buy in a high-growth area or an area with good rental yields so you can count on good cashflow?

First look at your budget parameters, then choose a great area for investment — somewhere offering good returns, somewhere that works for your strategy — which could be in any city or regional area in the country.

Wherever you're looking, find out about upcoming infrastructure and government spending. Seek out properties that outperform the averages. An investment-grade property may be in a school catchment zone, in a quiet street. Check you're not buying in a flood zone or under a flight path. Are there good shopping centres, universities, hospitals and transport connections in the neighbourhood?

HOW TO CHOOSE YOUR SEARCH AREA

First choose the macro area — the city, say. Then look at the suburbs within that city, and the streets within that suburb, to find the property that ticks all your boxes.

Many people imagine that all properties increase in value, but that's not so. It's really important that you buy in the right location and that you buy the right property there. This means doing your research: identifying the areas with good amenities and where the government is spending money on new infrastructure, looking at population growth and jobs growth, and focusing on markets that are more susceptible to large-cycle growth, such as Sydney and Melbourne.

👀 GOVERNMENT SPENDING AND INFRASTRUCTURE

State and council websites can give you information on any infrastructure that's being developed in areas where you're considering investing.

If you can find a town or suburb with good amenities, where the government is spending money on infrastructure, you have yourself a potential growth area. But you need to get into that sort of area early so you can capitalise on that growth.

Look at what infrastructure is already in place and what is planned for the future, such as sporting facilities for the Olympics coming to Brisbane in 2032.

For example, I bought a few properties in Western Sydney for clients before the Western Sydney International (Nancy Bird) Airport was signed off on. The airport has been in the pipeline for about 50 years and, at the time of writing, it's still in the early stages of being built. However, land prices are rising in areas like Badgerys Creek and surrounding suburbs, and they've been increasing ever since the airport was signed off.

As another example, the light rail was still in the pipeline when we moved into our house in Lewisham. During the time we lived there, however, the line was completed, which saw property prices in the area skyrocket. And another: The Newcastle light rail opened in early 2019, which is one reason why the Newcastle property market has also skyrocketed in the past few years.

So it's important to monitor where the government's putting its money and then try to invest there before everyone else does. It's easy to predict these new projects once they've been signed off and the government stipulates when they'll happen. That said, governments do often run late, so you may have more time than you think.

If you act on your knowledge that something is definitely *going* to happen, it's not a gamble.

 GENTRIFICATION

We all know an area that was once regarded as undesirable but is now hot property. Gentrification refers to the transformation of a suburb from an ugly duckling into a desirable swan. This happens primarily through the upgrading of the area's buildings and streets, shops and businesses, new developments, and the removal of any Housing Commission dwellings that may exist there.

There are ways of finding out if a certain area is about to be gentrified. It's likely to be signalled by the appearance of some good development projects in the area. Get in and invest there *before* those projects happen so you can capitalise on that growth. There's no point in buying in an area like that *after* it's happened, because you've missed out on the growth.

DEVELOPMENT APPROVALS

I've discussed the impact of major government developments, such as the airport to be built in Western Sydney, but there are other things to consider when researching what a local or regional council has planned. It's important to know what the neighbourhood is going to look like in the future, as well as the impact of any developments on the property you're looking at.

Some developments — hospital expansions; road, bridge or transport upgrades; new schools or shopping centres — likely will be of great benefit to your property, boosting the 'convenience factor' and adding value.

Some development approvals, however, signal that your property will soon sit next door to a major roadway, or that you'll lose your beautiful views because of the construction of an apartment block next door, or that you can look forward to a long period of noisy construction right outside your bedroom window.

JOB CREATION

How many jobs is the new development or infrastructure project likely to create for the area? You need to see rising employment.

$500 000 TO INVEST

In chapter 9, I talked about some of the options for someone with a million dollars to invest. For an investor with $500 000 to spend, Armidale in regional NSW is my first suggestion because it ticks all of the due diligence boxes I have listed.

The growth of Armidale's economy is driven by two big institutions: the University of New England and Armidale Hospital. In 2021 the $60 million dollar Armidale Hospital redevelopment was completed. Armidale's strategic location between Sydney and Brisbane, its population of well-paid professionals working at the university and hospital, and its own airport are all factors that should bring strong growth and rental yields in the years to come.

I also like other regional NSW hubs, including Orange, Albury and the Hunter region, as well as coastal locations such as Port Macquarie, Nambucca Heads and Merimbula in NSW and Geelong in Victoria — all of which I see as following in the footsteps of huge growth regions such as Lennox Head and Byron Bay, which are so popular with people moving away from the city for lifestyle reasons.

With an investment budget of $1 million, NSW Central Coast suburbs such as Lakehaven, Umina and Wyong also meet my due diligence criteria. Nearby Ettalong Beach has seen more than 38 per cent growth in the past five years and we can expect a ripple effect into surrounding areas.

With $1 million to spend, if you moved to Brisbane you'd be able to buy closer to the city and get yourself a house, so you wouldn't need to enter the unit market.

HOW YOUR STRATEGY IS IMPACTED BY LOCATION

It's easy enough to find a home for you or a tenant to live in, but finding the *right* property, one that works with your strategy; something you can perhaps subdivide or put a granny flat on — that takes a lot more due diligence. You've got to speak with town planners and with council and carefully check out the property itself to make sure there are no problems with easements, sewer lines and the like. For more on getting a development application (DA) through council, I explain the development process in detail in my book, *Positively Geared*.

👀 ENVIRONMENTAL RISKS

Before purchasing a property, it's important to know whether the property lies in an area vulnerable to bushfires, floods or other environmental risks.

BUSHFIRES

When searching for property, it's increasingly common to come across bushfire-prone properties, especially if they are regional or in new housing developments that have been established in forested areas. You can check whether a property is in a bushfire-prone zone on the Section 10.7 (zoning) certificate, or state equivalent, which forms part of your contract of sale. Be aware that some banks may not lend on bushfire-prone properties.

When developing in bushfire zones, the property will need to meet certain standards, including specific construction requirements. If you are planning any development or even renovations, it may be costlier than usual to ensure you meet council requirements, so look into this early on.

You may also find that your insurance premiums are higher because of the added risk your property carries, so you need to assess the impact of this on your bottom line.

FLOODS

Similarly, check whether the property is in a flood zone. Flooding in the area may be minor, moderate or major. The fact that the property is susceptible to flood damage means increased risk for the lender. Unfortunately, many flood-zone properties are not covered by property insurance, and appropriate flood-protection premiums can be very expensive.

Also, if you're planning on developing or renovating, the local council may not approve your plans or may impose additional hoops for you to jump through before approving your DA, which will come at an additional cost to you.

🔭 CRIME RATES IN THE AREA

When buying a property, it's important that you understand the character of the neighbourhood where you're planning to live or invest.

Crime rates vary significantly between suburbs. The crime statistics most likely to impact you, your tenants or your property's value are: break and enter, motor-vehicle theft, malicious damage to residential property, juvenile crime intent and drug trafficking.

Buying a property in an area with a high crime rate could end up costing you in the long term in repairs or insurance, whether you're going to live in the property or use it as an investment vehicle. You also need to ensure you're attracting the right kinds of tenants, so buying in the right area is crucial. Tenants will usually be willing to pay more to live in an area where they feel safe, so choosing to buy in a safe area will improve your cashflow and returns on the property.

Buying a property in an area with a high crime rate could also impact the future value of your property when it comes to selling, as owner-occupiers who will pay the higher purchase price typically prefer to live in a safe neighbourhood.

THE PROPERTY HUNT

Now you've found the right market through due diligence, I have a few tips on finding the right property for true market value.

As I noted in chapter 4, market value is not the current listing price or the amount for the most recent sale of the property. The market value of a property is the amount a willing buyer and a willing seller negotiate on any given day.

ABOVE MARKET VALUE

When a buyer pays much more than the market value of a property, this is referred to as 'overcapitalising' on a property, which means they risk not being able to make their money back if they immediately sell. Usually, overcapitalising will correct itself over the long term, through capital growth. However, this correction depends on how overcapitalised the property is, market growth and the property's location.

BELOW MARKET VALUE

A buyer who pays under the perceived market value of a property may have made instant equity on the property, meaning that the valuation of the property is greater than the amount the buyer paid.

Investors should always aim to purchase under market value, so as to create instant equity and make a profit from day one. Quite often they will use this additional equity to continue building their portfolio.

LLOYD'S STRATEGY

Buy at under the market value and *make money when you buy*, not just when you sell.

WHERE TO LOOK FOR BELOW-MARKET-VALUE PROPERTIES

I've mentioned that a lot of the properties I find are off market, and I learn about them through real estate agents I know. Here are a few ways you may obtain a property for less than its market value.

A DISTRESSED SELLER

A seller may be distressed for a number of reasons. Maybe they have lost their job and can no longer afford their mortgage repayments, so they need a quick sale. Or they may be a developer who has big bills to pay and needs to sell the property fast to pay outstanding debt. Whatever

194

the reason, a distressed seller usually needs the money from the property urgently, so you can secure a real bargain here if you are able to negotiate on short settlement terms.

This tip comes with a *buyer beware* warning: some sellers may want to sell fast because they realise there are issues with the property that they hope a buyer will overlook thanks to the excellent price tag and speedy settlement terms.

This is why it's always advisable to view the property in person and obtain an inspection report from a qualified building and pest inspector before purchasing. For apartments, it is important to review the strata reports and minutes from strata meetings thoroughly for evidence of any building defects, and to check the balance of the body corporate and sinking fund. Be cautious about buying into any building where the body corporate has spent significant funds on repairs. And always have your solicitor or conveyancer check all contracts for properties you intend to buy.

NEGOTIATE THE TERMS OF THE CONTRACT

In many instances, a buyer will purchase a new home before selling their current home. This means they rely on selling their current home to settle on their next one, which locks them in to a strict time frame for selling their current home or they risk defaulting on payment for their new home.

Bear in mind that sellers may allow a substantial negotiation on their property if they've already purchased their next home and are running out of time before the pre-settlement period on their new property ends.

If you can be flexible on the settlement terms of your contract, this can put you a head above other potential buyers, as flexibility is a strong negotiation tool to bring to the table. If you are able to settle in as little as 21 days instead of the standard 35 or 42 days, you could find yourself getting a much better deal on the property.

PATIENCE

No matter what the market conditions, there will always be sellers who are either distressed or in need of specific settlement terms. If you have the patience and are able to negotiate on some of the purchase terms, you may find yourself securing a really good property at below its market value.

WHERE TO START YOUR SEARCH

When I'm doing research to look for properties, especially if it's in a city I don't know very well, I spend a lot of time with government sources such as council websites and property intelligence sites like CoreLogic and Pricefinder. Some of these are paid sites, some are free.

But while online research is helpful, there's a limit to what you can learn on a computer. There's nothing like actually going to an area and pounding the pavement and talking to locals to find out whether the area is really a good place to invest in.

If you can't travel, getting a friend to speak to locals on your behalf can be a great way to get a feel for an area. Asking property managers and real estate agents who live and work in the area is also useful.

Here are some things to check out:

- **Population growth.** If you want to see growth in property values, look in areas where there's good population growth. I also usually only buy in areas that have a population of more than 20 000 in the first place.
- **Several industries.** Make sure you're buying into an area that has *many* drivers of economic growth, where the local economy is underpinned by several industries that help drive growth in that town, so if one of those industries collapses, others will keep the town moving forward.
- **Property value increases.** Look for an area that has seen property prices rise by at least 6 or 7 per cent in the past decade.

This may not seem like a lot of growth but we're talking about averaging it out over a period of 10 years; most capital cities will have higher growth than this. Look at property prices in the past 12 months, then look back two years and five years. In a booming market, the area could have seen 20 or 30 per cent capital growth over the past 12 months, but growth over 10 years might have been only 5 per cent per annum. This is why you need to look at historical growth figures as well as recent ones. You don't really want to buy into a booming market; as I've mentioned in earlier chapters, ideally you want to get into an area *before* it takes off.

- **Amenities.** Good overall house price growth in a market doesn't mean that all properties there will increase in value at the same rate. You've got to buy the right property for the right demographic, making sure it's close to the amenities that the local residents demand.

  I spend a lot of time checking the amenities and services that are available in an area. People much prefer to live in well-located homes — in a school catchment zone, on a quiet street, near a park or water, close to shopping and transport amenities. Depending on what you or your future tenants need, you might be looking at homes that are close to train stations, schools, a university or a hospital.

- **Demographics.** Buying the right property for the demographic of the area is also important. Look at the types of people who live in the neighbourhood or are moving into the area, and what kind of homes they like to live in, as well as whether they like to own or rent.

  If you're buying an investment property in, say, Campbelltown in south-west Sydney, you don't really want to be buying a one-bedroom unit when most people in the area are families who live in four- or five-bedroom houses. That's an example of buying the wrong property in the wrong location.

I also advise buying into an area with a high proportion of owner-occupiers to renters, as this indicates greater stability in the community. Also, most owners take more pride in their properties than do renters, and are more likely to spend money on upkeep, which pushes up the value of the neighbourhood.

THE RENTAL MARKET

If you're buying an investment property, you need to look at rental markets to find figures on the following fundamentals:

- **Owners and renters**. I look for a ratio of around 75 per cent owner-occupiers to 25 per cent renters in the market. At 25 per cent, there are enough potential renters to enable you to rent out the property, but owner-occupiers, the people who really drive growth, predominate in the neighbourhood.

- **Vacancy rates**. One of the most important things to look for in rental markets is vacancy rates. I always try to invest in areas that have vacancy rates of less than 3 per cent (which is considered equilibrium), and prefer 1 to 2 per cent.

- **Rental return**. Rental return is the total rental income divided by the property purchase price; multiply that figure by 100 to get the percentage yield. For example, if you have a million-dollar property and you're bringing in $52 000 a year in rental income, you have a 5.2 per cent yield, which is considered neutral. If you're looking for a positively geared property, you need a yield of 6 per cent or more. An investor on a higher income might be comfortable with a negatively geared property in a high-growth area, so 4 to 4.5 per cent might satisfy them.

INSPECTING PROPERTIES

It is really important to view the property before you buy. There's nothing like being on the ground yourself. But if you can't get to the property, engaging a buyer's agent to do it for you can save you a lot of time, money and legwork. And we do that kind of stuff all the time.

When I'm buying for clients, once we've short-listed the properties we're interested in, we go and check them out, beginning with their street appeal.

You may have thought the place looks okay online, but now you find out it's actually not in a great location. It's on a noisy road, or you turn up and you find a building site or what looks like a drug lab next door. I always drive by at night as well, to make sure it's a quiet street.

PSYCHOLOGY BEHIND AUCTIONS: TIPS TO WINNING

When you've found your property and you're ready to make an offer, make sure it's a serious one (as discussed in chapter 6), and make sure you're prepared.

If you're going to auction, I recommend using a buyer's agent for purchasing your own home. But if you're going to bid at auction yourself, I have some tips for you.

So how can you bid like a professional at auction and give yourself the best chance of winning?

SET THE PACE OF THE AUCTION

Auctions are known to move very fast, and there are good reasons for this. Fast-moving auctions make you feel like you're in danger of missing out, so you place a bid before the property is ripped out from under you. But it doesn't need to be like that.

There are many advantages to setting the pace of an auction yourself. It shows you are in control, and other bidders may start to feel at a disadvantage as they see you becoming the focus at the auction.

At the start of an auction the auctioneer will usually recommend a price increment—for example, they may request round-number bids of $20000 or $10000 increments. This is because throughout the auction, the auctioneer needs to add up the numbers in their head very quickly before carrying on to the next bid while also keeping up the pace, excitement and momentum of the auction.

If you were to throw in a bid of a different increment — say, $8250 instead of $10 000, or $3400 instead of $5000, this will slow the pace of the auction as the auctioneer struggles to add up the numbers. Altering the pace of the auction is one way a bidder can start to control an auction.

🔲 GIVE THE APPEARANCE OF AN UNLIMITED BUDGET

I've talked about how I give nothing away at auction by wearing my poker face and showing no emotion. To give yourself the best chance at an auction, my top tip is to give the impression to other bidders that you have an unlimited budget, no matter how hard they try and what bid they put in. This can demotivate other bidders, putting you in a winning position.

No matter what other bidders throw out, if you counterbid *immediately* they often start to get nervous and discouraged, and begin believing they have no chance.

Even if you're nearing the top of your budget, continue to act confidently and offer counterbids in quick succession, even if they're just $1000. Your confidence may convince your opponent that there's no point in bidding further, because you'll just keep on coming back with another counteroffer. It's vitally important that you remain confident *right up to your limit*, so the other bidders have no clue that you're close to your maximum.

WHEN YOU'VE WON: THE COOLING-OFF PERIOD

You've finally found your ideal property, made your offer and had it accepted. Congratulations! Before you break out the champagne, though, it's worth thinking about how you're going to use the cooling-off period to ensure you're still celebrating when you finally take possession of the keys.

Of course, when buying at auction there's no cooling-off period, but for other buyers it's a chance to get your finance formally approved before going unconditional. In fact, there's a whole lot more you can (and should) do at this time.

1. CONDUCT A BUILDING AND PEST INSPECTION

In a hot market, many buyers are rushing in and making offers — often 'sight unseen' — without knowing exactly what they're getting for their money. If that's you, then as soon as you've had your offer accepted, make sure you line up a building and pest inspection as early as possible.

If you've already had an inspection done before buying, but something in the report is keeping you up at night, now is the time to send someone in for a closer look. For example, your pest report may indicate signs of previous termite activity on the property. To play it safe, use the cooling-off period to organise a more thorough termite inspection to make certain there are no active pests on the property.

2. GET QUOTES FOR ANY WORK THAT NEEDS TO BE DONE

Take your time going through the building report, noting in particular any defects or urgent repairs recommended by the inspector.

It can be tempting to turn a blind eye to issues raised in the report. But as you'll see in the next point, it really pays to get accurate quotes for any work that needs to be done on your property.

If the guttering looks like it will have to be replaced soon and the bathroom is showing signs of water damage, plus there's a suspicious crack in the living room, send a builder in to give you an accurate estimate of the cost of repairs.

Investing wisely is all about getting the numbers right. Sometimes it's even worth losing your holding deposit and backing out of a deal if the numbers don't stack up.

Call the building inspector who did the inspection to discuss the report in more detail so you have a clear idea of the property's condition, as a report by itself might not present the full story, or it could sound worse than it is.

🏠 3. NEGOTIATE THE FINAL SELLING PRICE

The good news is, there is room for negotiation on the selling price right up until end of the cooling-off period, provided you have a fair reason.

Perhaps you've discovered that the water damage mentioned in the building report signals a more serious problem, and your builder has estimated the work is going to cost $10 000 and must take place within the next few months.

At this point, you may consider pulling out of the deal — or you can go back to the vendor and ask for a reduction in the selling price. This stratagem may be less effective in a seller's market, but it's always worth asking, as a motivated vendor may be willing to give ground in order to lock in the sale and continue pushing towards settlement.

🏠 4. ASK ALL THE QUESTIONS YOU DIDN'T HAVE TIME FOR EARLIER

During the cooling-off period, make sure you take a breath and revisit some important questions:

- Have I considered issues like fire and flood risk?
- Has my solicitor found any potential concerns with the contract?
- What is the neighbourhood really like?
- Would I be better off backing out now and looking for a more suitable property?
- Is the property truly aligned with my long-term investment strategy?
- Is the rental estimate provided accurate?
- Do the numbers stack up in terms of generating the cashflow I need?

Answering these questions honestly should give you peace of mind, knowing you've made a great purchase that will serve you well for years to come.

5. EXTENDING YOUR COOLING-OFF PERIOD

If you're running out of time for getting the answers you need, it may be possible to have the cooling-off period extended.

Extending the cooling-off period is completely at the vendor's discretion, but they may be willing to be flexible, especially if you need just another day or two to get your loan approved or you have identified a major issue that will most likely also be raised by any subsequent prospective buyer.

LLOYD'S STRATEGY

Keep a buffer of 5 to 7 per cent of the purchase price.

YOUR BUFFER ZONE

I always recommend you maintain a financial buffer, an extra 5 to 7 per cent on top of the purchase price, so you aren't paying more than you can afford to on a property. This is useful in case bank valuations come in short or you need to do repairs on the property.

Also, if you want to buy a property, and plan to leverage some equity off it to buy another, then the value of the initial property actually *falls* so you don't get that equity, having the buffer will allow you to go forward with the other property anyway.

So it's a contingency plan, but ultimately the key is to make sure you're getting into a good market to start with, and that confidence comes from doing all the research up front.

RENTING OUT A PROPERTY

If you've bought an investment property in a good growth area with low vacancy rates and you've done your research, you probably already know how much rent to expect. Some property owners tend to be a little greedy for rent. If it's suggested to them that the market rate is $400 a week, some landlords will want more, so they'll put $420 on it and end up not renting it out. Or, if it's a softer time of the year in the rental market, and they might be better off advertising it for $380, they insist on $400.

The problem is that if they don't rent it out at all, they're actually *losing* $380 a week, as opposed to losing just $20 a week by reducing the rent by that amount.

I watch the rental market. I also take advice from my property managers and if they suggest I should rent a property for a certain amount, I go with that, without being greedy and without trying to squeeze out another $5 or $10 or $20 a week if that's likely to put the tenancy at risk.

Rentals typically (though not always) move in the same direction as property values in the market, so they can actually decline if the market really declines. For example, I paid about $260 000 for my 'big mistake' property in the Queensland mining town of Blackwater. At the time it was renting for $800 a week, which delivered a massive yield. When the market collapsed there, it ended up renting for just $200 a week.

Fortunately, I had bought only one property in a mining town, but I certainly learned from that experience. My portfolio is built on investments in areas that have multiple economic growth drivers in place.

Keep in mind the time of the year when renting out a property. For example, it's potentially trickier to rent your property, or at least to get a premium rent for it, in winter. So if you need to launch a rental in those months, you might have to ask a bit less for it to secure a tenant.

In that situation I recommend offering a six-month lease, then readvertising in the summer months at a higher rental, or increase the rent with the current tenants after the first six months. Alternatively, you can give tenants a 12-month lease but have a clause written into the contract that specifies a $10 a week increase after six months.

It's often easier to secure tenants in autumn, spring, or summer. Keep in mind, though, that it can become difficult close to the Christmas/New Year break. If you're renting out a property in an area near a university,

February is a better time to rent, as that's when the first semester starts. So keep in mind when prospective tenants will likely be looking.

I have more advice for landlords in my book, *Positively Geared*.

CASE STUDY
UNDER MARKET VALUE WITH $200K+ DEVELOPMENT PROFIT POTENTIAL

A lovely young couple in their twenties, Jane and Dave, came to us looking to buy an investment property in Newcastle. As they were both working interstate in the mines, their time was quite limited and they had been restricted to inspecting properties on their days off, when they could fly in. This was costing them a lot of money on airfares as well as using up all their free time.

Jane and Dave have a much larger long-term goal than buying just one property. They want to start building up a property portfolio *now* so they can enjoy life early on rather than having to wait until retirement age to do so.

After meeting with them in Newcastle to discuss their strategy, we decided to search for a property in a high-growth area that would also offer Jane and Dave value-adding opportunities or future development potential. This would allow them to create instant equity and progress more quickly towards their goal.

THE LOCATION

With family living in Newcastle, Jane and Dave knew the area quite well and had done quite a bit of research on the market too. We were also very familiar with this market, having had many clients successfully purchase and build duplexes there recently.

Our goal here was to focus on high-growth suburbs in close proximity to the CBD, transport links, shopping centres, schools and other amenities. We also had to make sure the property was in an area with high rental demand and low vacancy rates.

(continued)

DUE DILIGENCE

After a number of weeks of searching and inspecting properties, we found one that ticked all the boxes. The property was well presented already, meaning it would be rent-ready from day one, and it was in the council's R3 zoning, which meant there was further scope to add value.

After meeting with Newcastle Council's town planner to discuss what options we had with this block, we spoke with a surveyor to calculate the costs involved in doing a subdivision, and with a builder to determine the approximate cost of the build. With our dream team development experts, we were able to prepare a feasibility report around all the numbers, which indicated a potential development profit of $200k+.

Not only would Jane and Dave be capitalising on the existing dwelling in this high-growth suburb, but they also had the opportunity to create instant equity when they were ready. This was going to allow them to build up their property portfolio much faster than simply buying and holding could.

NEGOTIATIONS AND ACQUISITION

This property was set to go to auction a week after we commenced our negotiations, so it was important to make sure we had everything ready to go, from doing all of our due diligence to organising the building and pest report, getting the solicitor to review the reports and contract, and requesting any necessary amendments. Only a few days out from auction day, time was tight.

Then the agent called to advise that he had received a slightly higher offer than ours but that the vendors were happy to proceed with Jane and Dave's offer and sell it prior to auction, as we had already prepared everything and were ready to exchange.

It pays to be organised!

THE NUMBERS

Purchase price:	$663 500
Stamp duty:	$0*
Legals:	$1900
Building and Pest Inspection:	$550
TOTAL PURCHASE COSTS:	**$665 950**
Vacancy rate:	0.7%
Annual growth:	19%

*No stamp duty because of government grants for under $700k purchase price.

CASE STUDY
THE HIGHEST OFFER DOESN'T ALWAYS WIN

For the clients in this case study, offering better terms was the winning strategy.

Amy and Greg lived interstate and, with a healthy budget of $4 million, they wanted to relocate to a dream home on Sydney's beautiful Northern Beaches.

Both of them worked full-time so they lacked the time to search, do their due diligence and negotiate. And as they lived thousands of kilometres away, it was impossible for them to attend open homes, meet with agents and engage with what was happening in the local market. So they hired me to help.

THE CHALLENGES

To find their family home, I needed to build up an understanding of what was really important to them. What would their future in this home look like? Through their wish list, we ascertained what Amy and Greg saw as essential attributes of the property, and what they were willing to compromise on. The picture we built up would help us find them a really good home in the suburb they wanted.

(continued)

We personally inspected more than 20 properties in the key suburbs we'd pinpointed, and presented Amy and Greg with a shortlist of properties that met their specific criteria.

We showed Amy and Greg the shortlisted homes by using our virtual property inspection service, by which I took them through the property in a live viewing and they were able to ask any questions they had while I was right there on site.

THE RESULT

Aided by our relationships with local agents, we were able to present to Amy and Greg a beautiful property in their favourite suburb that was off-market. This meant that Amy and Greg had an advantage over other buyers in the market because they had first-look access to a property that had yet to be listed.

But with the Sydney market moving fast, the owners of the property ended up deciding to list the property before our clients gave the go-ahead for us to put forward an offer. By the time Amy and Greg were ready, we discovered that the situation had changed and there were now eight other offers on the table.

To give Amy and Greg a competitive advantage, we ensured they had finance approval as well as offering a higher deposit to show how committed they were to buying this beautiful home for their family. We also negotiated a shorter settlement period, which was advantageous to the sellers.

Although Amy and Greg did not put forward the highest offer, the seller preferred the terms of our purchase over those offered by the other prospective buyers, which meant we successfully secured Amy and Greg's dream home at an excellent price of $3.65 million.

THE WINNING TERMS

Amy and Greg were in a strong financial position. We checked with the bank to see if we could settle in less than the usual 42 days. We put forward an offer that included a 21-day settlement. As the vendors needed to sell and move quickly because they had bought elsewhere, this worked well for them. I had also advised Amy and Greg to pay their 10 per cent deposit into the agent's trust account as soon as our offer was accepted, even before the contracts were signed. This showed our serious intent, and 21 days later the home was officially theirs.

CHAPTER 11

THE FREEDOM PLAN

As your portfolio sees more growth and cashflow, debt can vanish forever

We've talked a lot about lifestyle goals and achieving those goals through property investment. Now let's look beyond that to achieving financial freedom, which might be defined as freedom from debt plus a sustainable passive income generated through an investment property portfolio.

THE INVESTMENT CYCLE

There are three phases to a property purchase: acquisition, hold (for growth) and sell (or exit):

» **Phase 1: Acquisition.** Your first step is to decide on a starting point based on your budget and to locate the kind of property that will support your strategy—one in a high-growth area that offers excellent cashflow.

» **Phase 2: Hold.** In this phase, you'll decide whether to hold the property for long-term growth or to sell it for a medium-term return.

» **Phase 3: Exit.** Once you've achieved the interim goals in the strategy, you need to plan your exit strategy for the property and some of the other properties you hold.

PLANNING YOUR EXIT STRATEGY

One aspect of building an investment portfolio I have touched on thoughout *Buy Now* is the need to put in place a long-term *exit strategy*, which is all about looking at what properties you can sell, then paying off all your debt — because at some stage you will need to actually pay off all your debt.

As you know, whenever I talk to anyone about investment strategy, whether or not they come to me as a client, I tell them it all starts with a question: 'Where do you want to be in the future?'

You've got the hang of this now — so what does the future look like for you? Do you want to retire in 10 years with a passive income of $100 000, or put the kids through private school, or pay off your home? Once you have established the goals most important to you, *then* you build a property investment strategy to help you achieve them.

And because you've read this book, you may decide, 'Okay, I need to buy properties in growth areas, properties that are or will become cashflow-positive'. Or you may think, 'I need to add value to these properties through subdivision or renovation or building a granny flat or some other kind of development'.

I talk through this strategy with every client I meet with. Once the first property is decided, we can plan what the second property will be, and the third property — and so on.

But what a lot of people miss, and what in many cases prevents them from reaching their end goal, is that *all debt needs to be paid off*, because you can't actually have passive income from properties if it's all attached to debt.

Let's say your investment properties are paying you $25 000 a year on average in rental income. If you have eight rental properties, each of which pays $25 000, you're making $200 000 a year in rent. But if you're also carrying $200 000 in mortgages per year, every time your rent comes in you have to use it to pay the interest on the mortgages as well as your other expenses, so you're not making any passive income and you'll be left without any cashflow.

Your goal has to be to build up enough equity to *pay off* that debt.

WORKING TOWARD A FINANCIAL GOAL

To really home in on your exit strategy, we review your financial goal and when you want to retire.

In this book, as in *Positively Geared*, I have focused on attaining financial freedom through the strategy of setting up a passive income that clears $100 000 a year, because that's what a lot of my clients aspire to. I also explained in chapter 2, that to achieve that you actually need to be making more than $100 000, because you have to cover your expenses as a property owner.

To clear $100 000 a year you need a total rental income of around $175 000 a year. And you need a $3.5 million rental-property portfolio *paid off* to achieve that $100 000 annual income.

So in reality, having decided that you need six investment properties to achieve a passive income of $100 000, you might find you actually need 12 properties so you can sell half of them to pay off all your debt.

And that will work only if all the properties increase in value, whether through capital growth or through adding value via development or renovation. Either way, all your properties need to be appreciating.

This is where many people get stuck, thinking that all they need is positively geared properties with a really high rental return. But that's not what they need. What they really need is a high-growth property, because ultimately *it's growth that creates wealth*.

For example, if you buy a property with a high rental yield but it's in a low-growth area, you'll never achieve your goals. Buying the wrong type of property is one reason why many people don't achieve their goals, and I hope you have learned enough from this book to never make that mistake yourself.

The last few chapters were all about finding and buying properties in growth areas. From reading these chapters, you may have developed a few ideas for an investment strategy of your own, one that will help you attain your own goals.

CORRECTING INVESTMENT STRATEGIES

One of the most common issues budding property investors face is their failure to really plan how they'll continue to expand their portfolio. Clients come to me all the time looking for ways to correct their investment strategies. It always comes down to money.

The two biggest issues here are usually cashflow and borrowing capacity. Very often people start their property investing journey by investing in negatively geared properties that both weigh on their cashflow and hurt their serviceability.

Buying a negatively geared property may work for a high-income earner in terms of reducing their tax, but it doesn't help them continue to build their portfolio beyond a certain point. Unless their income is very high, after loaning them money for three or four investment properties, the banks will cut them off and their property portfolio will hit a wall.

Other clients come to me with a different problem: all their loans are cross-collateralised with one bank, which prevents them from progressing further. In order to move forward, we have to fix the financing that was set up poorly at the start.

Still others have simply bought the wrong properties — or, in some cases, just one property. It may be in a bad location so it's actually going down in value and they need to sell, even if at a loss, to be in a position to move forward and get positive cashflow in the future.

I have a lot of conversations with clients (like Tim, whom we'll meet in the following case study), in which we have to work out which of the investment properties they have are going to perform, and which we may have to let go so we can continue to move forward with their long-term strategy.

CASE STUDY

INVESTOR BUYS HIS FIRST SYDNEY PROPERTY AFTER A DUPLEX DEVELOPMENT

Tim already owned eight properties when he came to me. They were all regional properties so he had really good cashflow, and he'd been advised just to keep buying these regional properties. But after looking at his portfolio, I said, 'You're never going to get financially free this way. You're going to be one of those people who own 100 properties but still have to keep working!'

That's the problem. People talk about how many properties they have, but it means nothing if you're still in the rat-race—because by itself, all cashflow does is pay off the weekly loan on the property. If you don't get that capital growth over the long term, you can't really get ahead.

I counselled Tim, 'You're never going to get ahead because you're never going to get much growth on these regional properties'.

I started working with him on a strategy that would see him start to buy in capital cities instead of focusing solely on regional properties. Tim's a Sydney person but he'd never bought in Sydney. He was advised that the best type of property to buy was in regional areas where you find good rental yields for properties costing only $400 000. So he's got eight of them!

As you know, I recommend buying regional for those very reasons—if you *can't* buy in Sydney or Melbourne. But if you *can* afford to buy in those cities, of course you still should—as long as that suits your strategy.

Part of the strategy we developed with Tim was to do a duplex development first to generate some instant equity. So although Tim already had lots of regional investments, we bought him a property down on the NSW South Coast where we did a duplex development

(continued)

that produced a couple of hundred thousand in equity. Then he bought a property in Sydney. The South Coast duplex created enough equity to put Tim in a position where he was finally able to buy his first Sydney property.

The strategy with that Sydney property was that Tim would subdivide it then develop the back half while renting out the existing dwelling.

The next property we bought for Tim was in a high-growth area in the northern suburbs of Brisbane. It was on a large block, which could be subdivided. Tim can look at a couple of options there: developing the property down the track, or putting a granny flat on it for additional income. With a dual-income property in a high-growth area, he has the best of both worlds.

You won't find that kind of opportunity in many areas. And Tim is ecstatically happy, because although he's an experienced investor, these new strategies are already helping him move more quickly towards his goals. With the way the current markets are, he's going to make massive equity just by *owning* properties in Sydney and Brisbane.

DREAM TEAM: BUYER'S AGENTS

You may have picked up this book because your own investment property or portfolio has ground to a standstill. With a sound strategy, extensive research and preparation, and realistic expectations, dreams can come true. It's complicated, but if you need help you can always contact a buyer's agent, as we do this day in and day out.

HOW TO FIND A BUYER'S AGENT FOR YOUR DREAM TEAM

Buyer's agents can be found via online searches and word of mouth. Word of mouth is especially valuable if someone you know has used a buyer's agent and had a good experience with them.

BUYER'S AGENTS' FEES

Their fees vary for a number of reasons, including experience and the scope of work involved. (Is it an investment property, a development or a primary residence you are looking for?) Most will offer part or full services, or specific services such as appraisals, search and negotiate, and bidding at auction, and they will quote you depending on the service you need.

Buyer's agent fees can range from a few hundred for a basic service or appraisal to a few thousand for a full service.

There is great value in using the right buyer's agent. You need to ensure you are getting value for money and aligning yourself with an agent you can trust. Their job is to work for you, and their fee should be minimal in comparison to what it would cost you if you bought the wrong property.

Check that your buyer's agent is licensed in the state in which you wish to buy. They should also have professional indemnity insurance, so don't be afraid to ask.

WHAT A BUYER'S AGENT DOES

A buyer's agent will first build an understanding of their client's brief and set up a purchasing strategy. Many will also help their clients plan a long-term investment strategy.

First they will assess your wants and needs in relation to a home or investment property. Then they will provide you with pertinent information about your local housing market, source properties in line with your brief, and act as an intermediary between you and the listing agent to ensure a smooth real estate transaction. They will also schedule showings and attend open houses on your behalf.

Once you're ready to purchase, they will help you with budgeting, and help facilitate the purchase with your mortgage broker or bank. They can also bring in other members of their dream team, including an accountant and solicitor, and organise the building and pest inspection.

If needed, they will create documents such as representation contracts, purchase agreements, closing statements, deeds and leases to close the sale.

People ask for my advice as a buyer's agent. We'll talk about strategies, but the next piece of advice I give them before I begin sourcing property is to speak to a mortgage broker about finance, and speak to their accountant about the structure they should buy in as well as for tax advice. If they need assistance finding these professionals for their dream team, I can assist with the right contacts.

BECOMING DEBT FREE

As we discussed in chapter 3, the key to building up an investment portfolio is generally taking on interest-only loans (if your banks allow it), in which your payments cover only the interest on your mortgages. Your mortgage is generally no higher on an investment property, but the *value* is higher as the market grows over the years, so you'll actually be able to sell the properties at a profit, then to use that profit to pay down even more debt. That's how to use an exit strategy to achieve financial freedom faster. Of course, sometimes it is better for long-term portfolio growth to be paying both principal and interest. The alternative is to then try to pay off all your properties, including the principal. But if you sign up for a 30-year mortgage with the bank and you make only the minimum repayments, it's going to take you 30 years to pay it off.

Let's say you're 30, and you decide you're going to do it the old-fashioned way, and you want to retire when you're 70. Well, you *could* do it that way. You could actually own a whole lot of properties and just slowly pay them all off. But it's a really slow way of doing it that will keep you in the rat-race until you're 70.

The strategy I'm proposing is much quicker and frees you from the rat-race by having some properties paid off that give you cashflow.

The time it takes to pay off your debt depends on your circumstances. The more ambitious among you will want to retire when you're 40.

If you're 30 now, you're going to want to set up an exit strategy that will enable you to pay off all your debt in 10 years. But if you're 39 and you want to retire when you're 40, that's not going to happen. A decade is usually a pretty good time frame.

It also depends on your goals. Some people have realistic goals — for example, to achieve $50 000 or $80 000 in passive income within a decade. That can be done. But I recently received an email from someone who wants to achieve $300 000 in passive income within 10 years. That's not achievable, in my opinion, unless you're on an extremely high income and have already made a good start.

It depends on a lot of other variables too, including how savvy you are, your current income, what the banks will lend you and what you're willing to do. Quite often, people who have these grandiose ambitions end up not even making a start.

TIME TO SELL

If we do things my way, the goal is ultimately to have no debt attached to any of the properties in your portfolio.

When you sell down, you choose which properties to keep and which to put on the market. The properties you sell are those that will best help you pay off not just the debt on the properties themselves but your other debt too.

If you're building a duplex, for example, you'll decide whether you're going to hold both units, sell one or sell both. You might build the duplex and hold both units for cashflow and equity, but sell the whole duplex as part of your exit strategy 10 years down the track.

As you know, duplex development is a strategy I myself often use. At the time of writing, I have just bought another block of land down on the Sapphire Coast of NSW, near Merimbula, to build a duplex on. My strategy will be to keep one unit for cashflow and sell the other to further pay down our home in Lilli Pilli.

My investment strategies have enabled me to put chunks of the equity and profit I was making into the offset accounts to pay off my home loans, as explained in chapter 2. For example, I paid off my homes in Ingelburn and Lewisham completely through my investment strategies, and I'm currently paying off our Lilli Pilli home that way too. Although I signed up for 30-year loans — because that's what the banks offer you, and a 30-year loan means lower repayments — it hasn't taken me 30 years to pay off those loans.

I paid off my Lewisham mortgage in five years, but Lewisham was my *home,* not an investment property, so I didn't really have an exit strategy when I bought it, other than knowing I would live in a bigger place one day.

Usually you will keep an investment property longer if it has a higher yield and continues to enjoy good growth. But sometimes you reach a point where you think, well, now is a really good time to sell.

Because of the capital gains tax, I do generally keep my properties for long periods of time, but you can't keep all your properties forever. With multiple properties, it may be difficult to pay them all off by putting money into offset accounts, so selling to use the capital growth you've acquired on some properties is actually a good way to pay off the debt on *all* your properties.

CAPITAL GAINS TAX (CGT)

A capital gain, or capital loss, is the difference between what it cost you to obtain and improve the property (the cost base), and what you receive when you dispose of it. Amounts that you've claimed as a tax deduction, or that you can claim, are excluded from the property's cost base.

The cost base of a capital gains tax (CGT) asset is generally the cost of the asset when you bought it.

It also includes certain other costs associated with purchasing/acquiring, holding and selling/disposing of the asset.

This is why it is vital, when investing in a rental property, to keep records right from the start and work out what you can and can't claim as a deduction.

If you buy the property with someone else, you'll also need to work out how to divide the income and expenses.

If you make a net profit from renting your property, you may need to make pay as you go (PAYG) installments towards your expected tax liability. Generally, you only declare the income you earn from a property and claim related expenses if your name is on the title deed.

If you buy a property, the date you enter into the contract — not the settlement date — is your date of purchase for capital gains tax purposes.

Apart from buying, you can obtain a property by inheriting it, receiving it as a prize or gift, or having it transferred to you as a result of a divorce settlement.

Even if you have an investment property that is not rented or available for rent — such as a holiday home, hobby farm, or another property you choose not to rent:

- the property is subject to CGT in the same way as a rental property
- you generally can't claim income tax deductions for the costs of owning the property because it doesn't generate rental income
- you may be able to include your costs of ownership in the property's cost base, which would reduce any capital gains tax liability when you sell it.

If you acquired the property before CGT came into effect on 20 September 1985, you can disregard any capital gain or capital loss. However, you may make a capital gain or capital loss from growth improvements made since 20 September 1985, even if you acquired the property before that date.

WORKING WITH AN ACCOUNTANT WHEN SELLING A PROPERTY

Before you sell a property, have a conversation with your accountant about tax, because you need to understand what the tax implications are. You might think, well, the market's done pretty well—I'll make some money on this property.

If it's your own home, that's okay, because you don't have to pay capital gains tax on it, but if it's an investment property you want to sell, you probably won't be able to pocket all of the profit. Both the price it will likely sell for, and the type of entity it was purchased as, will affect the amount of capital gains tax you'll have to pay.

So having those conversations before you sell, and at every step of the way, will help you decide which properties from your portfolio to sell and which to hold.

UPSIZING TO YOUR DREAM HOME

The length of time you should hold your properties varies widely, because everyone's financial and life goals are different. What they're trying to achieve is different; even their 'dream home' goals are different. Some want to buy their own home; some just want to pay off their own mortgage.

Some people might be living in their dream home already, but they've got a big mortgage on it, and they want to be able to pay that off. One way to do so is to keep working for another 30 years while chipping away at the loan. A quicker, smarter way is to build up a portfolio of investment properties and use *them* to pay off the loan on their dream home.

I sold off a couple of properties to help buy our dream home in Lilli Pilli. Our Lewisham home was one of them and my strong investment property in Wallsend, Newcastle, was the other. I also used some of the profit from selling my former home in Ingleburn, which, after I lived in it, had served me well as an investment property.

When selling a property, most people just give most of the money back to the bank, but because I had already paid off Lewisham and Ingleburn, I got to keep the money, and that meant I had a large deposit to put down for Lilli Pilli. I bought Lilli Pilli for $4 million and just four years later, it was worth more than $6 million, thanks to good capital growth.

DOWNSIZING FROM YOUR DREAM HOME

Your dream home may be a part of your investment plan too. If you're downsizing because the kids have left home or you're retiring, then you're likely to be buying a cheaper property, so you'll probably have money left over.

I have occasionally helped people downsize to a townhouse or something similar, but there's no unique trick to that. It's more like they've got a five-bedroom house they don't need anymore because they're empty nesters, so they'll sell and downsize to something smaller.

This can work well for your retirement funds. Your family home might sell for a couple of million dollars, then you move into a low-maintenance unit for half the price. So you're in the happy situation of having $1 million more to fund your retirement. And if you don't blow that million on a new sports car or a boat, then you're not reliant on government payments or your kids if you live into your 100s.

CASE STUDY
DOWNSIZERS ACHIEVE $1M INCREASE IN EQUITY IN JUST THREE WEEKS!

John and Miriam are downsizers who sold their large family home in one of Sydney's most affluent suburbs, Vaucluse, in the eastern suburbs. They were hunting for a low-maintenance home where they could enjoy their retirement years, while remaining close to the local amenities of Double Bay and to the city.

(continued)

The property brief focused on a small search area in the inner east. It had to be suitable for them to be able to lock up and go off to their farm for extended periods of time without worrying about security or maintaining the gardens. John and Miriam had a budget of $9 million. This sounds high but is actually not a strong budget for the suburb they were looking in.

After searching for several months and constantly missing out on properties they liked, they decided to engage me as a buyer's agent.

THE CHALLENGES

When I first met with them, John and Miriam informed us that their settlement on the Vaucluse property was in 60 days, effectively giving us 30 days to find them their perfect property.

This was a near-impossible task given the fast-moving seller's market and the very tight search area. In fact, even in a 'normal' market this would be a big ask.

THE RESULT

Luckily, I have on my staff agents with expert knowledge of the eastern suburbs, and with our extensive real estate agent network, I was confident we would get the job done.

In just 18 days—a phenomenal feat in any market—we found our buyers their dream property in Darling Point. In fact, this was the first time in 10 years a property in this pocket of Darling Point had come onto the market.

However, like all A-grade properties in a tightly held pocket, there was very strong interest, including five other buyer's agents vying for the property. This is where our agent relationships and negotiation skills really came into play. My team was able to secure the property in a tense eight-hour negotiation. Even better, ours wasn't the highest offer on the night. Like a game of chess, it came down to strategy and reading the play.

We also secured the property for $2.5 million under John and Miriam's budget. And, by the time their Vaucluse property had settled, they were able to move in.

THE NUMBERS

Purchase price:	$6.5 million
Stamp duty:	$391 657
Legals:	$2500
TOTAL PURCHASE COSTS:	**$6 894 157**

The best news for John and Miriam was yet to come. Three weeks later, the apartment below the one we secured came onto the market. It sold in just three days for $1 million more than the property we secured for our buyers, at $7.5 million.

This extra million meant that a valuer would look at comparables and estimate John and Miriam's property at a million more, which meant our buyers had made $1 million in equity in just three weeks!

MY OWN RETIREMENT PLANS

Retirement means very different things to different people. For some, it's a lifestyle. For me, being financially free means having the time and financial ability to choose what I do and when I do it. It also means I can choose to help people. What I do nowadays combines my two passions: education and property. Through my books, podcasts and my agency, I am educating people about property and helping them to make solid, informed decisions.

I achieved financial independence at age 39, when the passive income from my property portfolio exceeded my annual teaching salary. So at age 40, I 'retired'. A couple of years after that, Renee and I bought our dream home. I'm still enthusiastic about growing my property portfolio, to ensure I continue to build that security and a legacy for Renee and our kids.

YES, I'M STILL FRUGAL

Money doesn't generally change people, especially if you've worked hard to acquire that money. It does bring out who you really are. To this day I remain frugal. I do now own a couple of nice cars and a boat, and things I used to not be able to afford and, back then, didn't even want. And of course, we live in a nice house.

I was fine about buying the dream home because that was for our family and was a big goal. When it came to the boat, I admit I hesitated. I thought, do I really need this? People who own boats rarely use them — everyone knows that!

But I knew it was important to reward myself for achieving my goals, and this was a reward. So, I thought, okay, how's my property portfolio been going? How has my business been going? How have I been going personally? Do I deserve it? Can I afford to spend money on this? And when I asked myself if I could afford it, I didn't mean did I have a spare few thousand in the bank? For me, it meant, *had my investments gone well lately?* And did I have a little extra — which was only a small percentage of what I've actually got saved to spend on investing — to spend instead on a 'luxury' purchase.

AND I'M STILL WORKING

In reality, since retiring, I work harder than ever — and I love it. It doesn't even feel like work. I'm often asked why I do what I do when I've achieved financial independence and many lifestyle goals already. The truth is I couldn't just sit on a beach and do nothing all day. That's okay for a holiday (especially if we buy the holiday home in Mollymook we have our eye on!), but I absolutely love work, and love being kept busy. And more important than that, I love helping and inspiring people to achieve their own lifestyle goals. I wanted to become a buyer's agent so I could help people achieve their dreams. That was the catalyst for starting Aus Property Professionals.

GIVING BACK

Being financially free also means you have the freedom to contribute to society in whatever ways you wish. One of the best things about having a positively geared property portfolio that delivers a good income is that it gives me the freedom to donate to charities. Some of the fees Aus Property Professionals receive from clients don't just go into the bank or back into the business. We give for the greater good as well.

For me, that means being able to donate to charities that are close to my heart, such as the Cancer Council, because we lost my father to the big C when I was a student, and to bushfire and flood appeals. In the future we want to develop plans to tackle world problems on a bigger scale through Aus Property Professionals through projects such as building homes and schools and helping with education in countries like Nepal.

I've seen firsthand how the kids in these places have nothing and yet are some of the happiest kids I've ever met. I want my own kids to see this, and to appreciate and enjoy what they have and not become spoiled.

It is important to me to contribute to society and to be helping people. And writing books helps me to achieve my goal of getting this message out there.

'If I can achieve financial freedom through property, so can you.'

I wasn't born with a silver spoon in my mouth. I started with not very much at all, and I was a very frugal, uncool twentysomething. But I had a goal, a passion really, and it took some time to achieve it. But I kept myself accountable and I kept my focus on that long-term goal, because I knew what I wanted. I strongly encourage you to do the same, to have a go. Even if you have little money in the bank right now, you can at least start to think about your *why* and to set a strategy for how you can save for that first deposit.

As the case studies you've read in this book illustrate, I genuinely help people every day, and I love doing it. It's exciting — it's what gets me up every morning to go to the office. I feel honoured by the trust clients place in me, and I find it deeply satisfying to see my clients achieve great results in property and progress towards their own goals. I'm always inspired by their dreams and helping fulfil them is something I take very seriously. And I take enormous pride in the results we achieve together.

Thank you for reading *Buy Now*, and I wish you all the very best as you pursue your goals and future endeavours.

One final piece of advice: All you really need to build wealth from property and realise those big life dreams is a strategy and self-belief. Keep yourself accountable and you will achieve your goals. Don't listen to the naysayers. And good luck!

If you'd like to get in touch with me, you can find me at:

- Base Camp Property Club:
  facebook.com/groups/basecamppropertyclub

- Aus Property Professionals:
  facebook.com/auspropertyprofessionals.com.au

- Website: auspropertyprofessionals.com.au

- Instagram: @auspropertyprofessionals

- Email: lloyd@auspropertyprofessionals.com.au

You can also listen to the Positively Geared Podcast on Apple Podcasts, Spotify, or wherever you listen to podcasts.

INDEX